The Divine Mirror of Loneliness

Susanne Mills

ISBN-13: 978-1539055846
ISBN-10: 1539055841

DEDICATION

I dedicate this book to the lonely people of the world. Alone is a context of existence. Lonely is a state of mind. Alone does not preclude or require lonely. Both are the result of choices we make.

CONTENTS

ACKNOWLEDGMENTS

A very special thanks to Toot and LeeRoy Young, my teachers and guides in and around the world of Columbia Beach, Whidbey Island and the little beach cottage I named "Creamsicle Cottage". Thank you also to my writing group, and their encouragement, without which I would have abandoned this book long ago. Also a special acknowledgment to the silent man who through his journals became my "divine mirror" and co-author of this book.

Cover and interior photos: Bryan Mills   www.bmillsphotography.com

1 ELEMENTS OF THE LESSON

Discovery

He left them behind, 51 years of journals so neatly recorded, tucked innocuously on the lower shelf of the microwave cart. I casually picked one up and flipped to a random page. As I read the entry, he stated, "*I found a blown 20 amp fuse this time. The refrigerator was off and the living room outlets also. The water in the ice trays had melted. I talked to LeeRoy Young for a couple minutes, that's one of the rare times anybody has talked to me, most of my life is in complete silence now.*"

That journal entry was dated March 20, 1999. To understand this depth of alone and loneliness, would be to understand a lifetime of disconnecting from interactions with people, relationships and the changing world. As I stood there with his journal in my hands, I could not reach that level of understanding, but I could begin. What he had penned in 51 years of journals allowed me to look for evidence, events and reasons that might show the sequence of disconnection and possibly why someone would close himself off from people, relationships and emotions. It would be my attempt to understand why someone would bury feelings so deep that there was rare evidence of their existence.

As I read the journals, it seemed that he functioned and communicated first and foremost in the tangible world. Over time he seemed to be restricting the world he was surrounded with to a narrowness that did not include people but rather tasks. Those tasks were broken down into numbers, dates, facts and figures. Up close and personal with the inanimate portion and at a distance from the human portion. Perhaps, at some point in time, only the tangible was allowed to enter his world.

As I reviewed the journals before me, the carefully penned thoughts and written documentation of a life, I flipped through the earlier pages, at previous entries, to see if there might be a thread of events.

Disconnecting

It happens a day at a time, the disconnecting. Over so many years, protective walls are built one course on top of another until the day arrives when the builder can no longer see over the top of the wall. Walls make it easier to handle life and keep the pain out. At least in the beginning it seems that way.

Relationships are messy, emotions can be raw and hurtful and feelings have to be dealt with. Many people never learn or understand how to deal with emotions and feelings. Instead, they deal with the messiness of relationships by pushing people away until those trying to connect with them get tired of trying and one day they simply do not come back. This avoidance becomes the coping mechanism of choice.

Most likely, one day he looked around inside the meticulous wall he so carefully built over decades of living and not living and he realized he was alone. In a room full of people, he was alone. Sitting in his little beach cottage that he loved so well, he was alone. He rarely spoke and most often chose to be by himself. I suspect it was easier that way. With the few people left in his world he was angry and felt somehow wronged. More pushing away.

On December 19, 1991 he said *" Lucille hasn't talked to me for a week. She thinks more of her old maid friends and miserable relatives than she thinks of me. I guess I've outlived my usefulness and she'll be glad when I'm out of the way."* Haven't we all said or thought something similar to that sentiment at times in our lives? Our kids don't come around or call as often as we would like, our spouse likes to spend time hunting, fishing, playing cards, shopping or visiting with friends and we find ourselves sitting alone. If we have not built walls around ourselves or at least not built them very high, we can more easily move past those thoughts of self pity into more positive thoughts and reconciliation. We have the ability to reach out and surround ourselves with friends, relatives, colleagues and activities that remind us that we are cared about and we matter in the world. When the walls are too high and we have successfully cut ourselves off from others, we do not get those messages of love, caring and connectedness. Thus the disconnection deepens and we have no idea how we might possibly change the circumstances we find ourselves in.

At one point late in his life I imagine he reflected back over the years as we humans are destined to do and he probably saw the signs. His heart might have softened to a sweet memory of his beloved wife in their early years, but it was too late. The walls were too high and she was gone. Everyone was gone. And so he counted the number of days it rained that season, recorded the number of inches of snowfall on Mt. Baker and noted the cost of a tarp from Fred Meyer. The tangible details of life were carefully printed in a series of journals as the years passed by. One day, totally alone after 88 years of life on this earth he slipped away as silently as possible so that no one would notice. I noticed.

Serendipity

I hadn't intended to notice, I mean it was such a serendipitous meeting - he and I. There are no accidents in this world. Nothing happens by chance - there is a reason to every happening on earth. That is the philosophy I live my life by and this meeting is further evidence supporting that belief. This story is about the intersection of a lonely man (I will call him Wilbur, Wil for short) and a 60-something, single career woman (myself), each moving through significant life transitions. These are my thoughts, observations and opinions. I will also share the thoughts of this man as recorded in his journal. I believe my purpose in this writing is to bring his voice and his joys and fears to life in combination with mine in order to deliver a poignant message about loneliness. This story allows Wil to communicate those things he never said aloud to a world with whom he rarely engaged in conversation. There is no fault to the happenings in this story, in his life or in mine. What happens or happened simply "is". We do the best we can with the skills and information we have at the time. Our life circumstances are just that and each day we have the opportunity to change what we are not happy with. Each day we have the opportunity to not add another brick to the wall we might find ourselves building.

Loneliness Is A Choice

It is an active decision to let people into our lives - we control the gates to our world - who comes in and who is kept out. In those decisions is the decision to be lonely or not. We choose to be lonely, it does not just happen. Many consider that quite a provocative statement and many believe it is not true. I disagree. Humans do choose to be lonely each and every day. A concept worth considering and understanding. This story is about an understanding of loneliness within the context of a life. An understanding which comes about as a result of reflection on one's own life and through observation of behavior or listening to the inner reflections of another - the "divine mirror" of life. What we observe in the behavior of others and in our reaction to that behavior is often and most always a reflection that our higher self wishes for us to know and understand. Through that mirror and the understanding it provides, we are able to grow and evolve into a more aware self. Thus the purpose of a "divine mirror".

A Gift From the Universe

Unexpected gifts from the universe. We are given gifts all the time, yet unless we are open, viewing through soft eyes - we will not recognize those gifts and they float right past us with just a hint of a whisper or a ripple through our consciousness. We spend most of our lives so busy in the "doing" of life that those gifts just disappear without even the slightest awareness from our conscious self that they were even there. I was given such a gift on March 31, 2012 in the middle of a rainy, cold Saturday afternoon.

On that day I bought a small beach cottage built in 1925. I actually won it at an auction! (More about that later). I had no idea what a significant impact that day would have upon how I would live my life from then on. I also did not realize the treasure contained within. The treasure is the history of the people who inhabited the cottage before it came to be in my possession and their message to me. I believe their message is meant to be shared so that others who find themselves living a lonely existence might understand how to escape into a life filled with joy, happiness and above all, filled with loving human relationships.

2 THOSE BEFORE ME

The cottage was inhabited by three significant people before me.
The first individual was a woman by the name of Berte Olson.
Born in 1882 in Stavanger, Norway, Berte Olson, a 9 year old girl
and her family became some of the early Scandinavian
homesteaders on Whidbey Island.

Berte became the very first female ferry boat captain in the state of
Washington. I came to know Berte through a storyteller, Jill
Johnson who researched Bertes' story and tells it with such talent
and detail, she makes Bertes' life come alive.

Berte was a very strong-willed woman. A woman of short stature
(less than 5 feet tall), living and working in a man's world in the
early 1900's. Having endured a hard childhood in poverty, she
learned to become a survivor. Berte lived in a cottage on Fidalgo
Island, the island sitting at the top of Whidbey Island and on which
the city of Anacortes is built. Berte and her husband owned and ran

a ferry route between Anacortes (Fidalgo Island) and Whidbey Island before the Deception Pass bridge was built. The fee for car and driver was 50 cents, with 10 cents additional for every extra passenger. "Extra large" cars paid 75 cents. Service was hourly, and the transit time was only five minutes. Patrons were cautioned that the schedule was "subject to storms, breakdowns, and conditions beyond our control." In 1935 the Public Works Administration (WPA) paid for a new bridge to connect Whidbey Island to Fidalgo Island and the mainland. With the completion of the bridge in 1935, the ferry route was put out of business. The marriage suffered the same fate, and Berte's husband Augie headed down south to work on the Steilacoom line.

an arial photo of the pass pre-bridge

Deception Pass Bridge

Being the survivor and entrepreneur that she was, Berte moved her ferry run over to connect folks to the Olympic Peninsula where the Hood Canal bridge now stands. One of the most amazing things that she did was to move her family from Dewey Beach (Fidalgo Island) to Hood Canal. She loaded all of their belongings into their cabin, loaded the cabin on a barge and took it with her.

Berte also barged a cabin down to the west side of Whidbey Island in 1940 and set it on Columbia Beach at the south end of Whidbey where a sister of hers already lived. Helena Olson, a different sister of Berte's moved into and lived in the cottage until a year before her death in 1955. It is unclear whether Helena bought it from Berte or it was simply given to her. The year before her death in July of 1954, Helena sold the cottage to a young couple from Kent, WA.

Berte Olson died in 1959 at age 77 in Seattle. Her ashes were scattered where the Hood Canal Bridge was built. The new bridge was in design phase from 1951-59 and completed in 1961 after

Berte's death. Berte never saw that bridge. Legend has it that the ghost of Berte Olson had something to do with why that bridge sank in 1979.

The second and third persons inhabiting the cottage before me were a married couple. Wilbur and Lucille Mills were in their late 20's and had a primary home in Kent, WA. This cottage would be their vacation home for 58 years. It was their retreat to a quieter life and activities such as fishing and golf. Both worked full-time jobs and although they together had no children, Lucille had a daughter named Maridel.

The neighbors I interviewed on Columbia Beach consistently described Wil as a very quiet man, one who stayed to himself most of the time and rarely engaged in conversation. They described Lucille as "very nice and very patient". Lucille had been dead over 10 years by the time I bought the cottage. Wilbur was still alive. As I sit and think about him I wish I had a face to put with his voice. I never met Wil and I would have been delighted to sit in conversation with the silent, tall man. It would have been lovely to hear him sharing the love for his fishing cottage and all things connected. That meeting was not to be. Wilbur died 1 month after I took possession of his beloved fishing cottage. He spent nearly 89 years on this earth. He owned his fishing cottage for 58 of those years. I believe he shared very little about himself with anyone - family, friends, co-workers, neighbors. One place, and perhaps the only place he shared thoughts consistently was in his journals.

3 THE JOURNALS

His voice, the notes and reflections of nearly 51 years were captured in five spiral-bound, lined notebooks of various sizes, colors and styles. Four were 8.5 x 11 in format with a metal spiral down the left-hand side, as was popular and used frequently for school or home. The first one has a price stamped on the cover of 25¢, the second one 39¢. Notebooks #3 and #4 have USB codes - a sign of the advancement in technology that came with the passage of time. The notebooks are faded and tattered with worn, faded edges, coffee mug stains, notations and mathematical calculations in pencil in various places. They appeared very commonplace - just some old notebooks, easily overlooked. I think that is why they were still there when I came along. Two were in the microwave cart, on a shelf just below the microwave and two were on a bedroom nightstand, under 5 or 6 Popular Science magazines dating back to 1952. They sat there, waiting under a layer of dust and old magazines. Waiting for me.

The journals as I found them

Wil's voice was carefully captured and penned, using block-style capital letters, very neatly written, almost how a professional engineer or architect would write. This made reading his journal writing very easy for me. It must have taken him a great amount of time to write so carefully. It seems Wil lived his life very carefully.

Wil used a journal-style format and it appears there was a journal entry for each day he spent in his fishing cottage between 1959 and 2010, a period of 51 years. The journey and voice contained within those carefully tended journals speaks very clearly to me and I believe his journey and message is meant to be shared. I surely did not have that awareness at the time I discovered the journals. After two years of careful consideration, reflection and conversation with others, I feel compelled to write this story, to open the door to his world so that you may walk the journey of this man. This was not an easy decision as I honor his life and feelings even though I never met him. I did change his name in the writing of this book although I don't think that makes any difference at all. I searched his name on the Internet and found nothing. Again, evidence of a life lived very quietly in a time that documented very little.

Perhaps you will imagine his voice, spoken at first through wonder and happiness with precise examination of occurrences in his life and then through loneliness, frustration, anger and sadness. Perhaps you will see the mirror of an opportunity for yourself to learn about yourself or about others in your life. The divine mirror at work, reflecting information and providing opportunities to learn

4 THE DESCENT INTO LONELINESS

His writing had very little content one might consider sensitive, emotional or in any way life-altering. His writings about reflections that could be perceived as from one's heart, or as thoughts expressed through or infused with any level of emotion or feelings were few in number. His journals contain what was important to him and most topics were very "safe" for him to write about - the weather, current events, the price of items bought, his repair and maintenance activities at the cottage and perhaps most important, the daily fishing report (size and species of fish, at what time, in what location using which lure). Over the years, his feelings crept in more and more. The passages become salted with frustration, resentment, then anger. Sadly, there was an increasing level of loneliness that crept into his entries. I think he needed an outlet for the sadness and the loneliness. His journals were that outlet and his anger was the expression of that loneliness.

I see Wil's writing as a "divine mirror" for myself and others. I believe his voice is a "divine mirror of loneliness", with a deep sadness and a lost ability to recover from that loneliness. Wil created his loneliness, a day at a time, over decades. As I read the journals I saw it building. In the beginning there were joyful, happy times highlighted in such entries about "his" fishing cottage, spending time fishing with his wife, attending to the cottage and accountings of his adventures at work. Times that he looked forward to. As the years passed, the joy was ever so slowly and surely replaced by frustration, judgment, resentment, anger, hostility and a descent into greater and greater loneliness. It did not happen overnight, it happened slowly, one missed opportunity at a time. Wil built the wall around himself very carefully, one brick at a time, over many years. He let fewer and fewer people into his world. His life was a world so painstakingly tended and it all existed behind the wall he built

The beginning of this book is intended to create a context so you might listen to his voice with greater understanding. There is much written between the lines, the part of his life that he did not dare write about or recognize on a conscious level. Certainly feelings that he did not want to make real on a piece of paper and give life to. As I share excerpts of his journal with you, as well as my journey through his world - both in his journals and in the fishing cottage he loved so well, I will illuminate with photos. My goal is that his memory has substance and some measure of permanence. It is a human hope that our lives have purpose and that we make a lasting contribution to this world. We hope that there is some lasting evidence that we lived and walked on this earth beyond our grave marker. I wish to assure some level of that memory for Wil and for myself.

Let me take you back to the beginning of this journey and my introduction to this silent man, the man I came to know through voice and evidence he left behind. Those details painted an image of a precise, logical, detail-oriented and very quiet man. The journey is more than two years old as I begin this writing and it continues to grow.

5 THE INTRODUCTION

The Pacific Northwest is the theater for all that transpires in this story, so to say it was a cold, rainy Saturday afternoon in March of 2012 on Whidbey Island, WA. would not be an unusual statement. What I experienced on that rainy day was unusual, in many ways.

Two weeks earlier, 85 year old Joan, a spry, sweet neighbor, told me about a beach cottage that was to be sold at an auction "down the street from me" as Joan shared. She was so excited and the way she shared the information let me know that she thought it was a very special and rare happening. She and I were both working as volunteers at the "Friends of the Library" book sale just up the street at the Community Center. I was a relatively new resident of Whidbey Island, having moved here a year before and did not understand the opportunity in her statement. I more-or-less said to myself "AND? - What does that have to do with me?" I had not expressed any intention to buy a beach home here or anywhere else.

Now this is where the story gets complex. I did have an unexpressed intention and desire to own a beach home. It has been a dream of mine for decades. The place where my children and their children - "THE grandchildren" come to visit. Grandparents call it "the magnet". Constructing a home at a destination where there is so much enjoyment that the grandchildren plead with their parents to go visit grandma (actually I'm called MoMo) and they come up to visit and you are privileged and thrilled to revel in their fun and adventures as a young family. If you are lucky, you build a relationship with your grandchildren and even, perhaps, rebuild a thinning relationship with your own children.

Sadly enough, so many parents and grandparents venture down that path - creating an irresistible draw or magnet (so they believe) where the family will visit and everyone can experience those memorable, wonderful times, those "Kodak®" moments. And guess what? It doesn't always work out that way. The camera is loaded but the subjects are missing. The visits are far and few between, the place sits empty and quiet. The beach balls sit deflated, the buckets and shovels gather dust on the porch and thoughts of doubt and loneliness, "no one cares" burrow their way into your thinking.

When I am truly honest with myself, I admit that I have had those thoughts on more than one occasion over a period of several years. Maybe the number of years coincide with the number of years my children have been on their own? Those thoughts of feeling alone, feeling as if you are not a part of your children's lives anymore, not being needed, are pretty normal and in the beginning, they were fleeting. They would be a flash on my radar screen, soon gone. However, as time went by and my life became quieter and theirs became busier, those thoughts were more frequent. I think of the song by Harry Chapin "Cat's In the Cradle" and it helps me realize it is a pretty common progression of thought and feeling for a parent:

> **I've long since retired, my son's moved away**
> **I called him up just the other day**
> **I said, "I'd like to see you if you don't mind"**
> **He said, "I'd love to, Dad, if I can find the time**
> **You see my new job's a hassle and kids have the flu**
> **But it's sure nice talking to you, Dad**
> **It's been sure nice talking to you"**

Even my two sisters were becoming distant, the road between our houses only being traveled a few times a year. Phone exchanges dwindled. Our lives seemed to be on separate paths.

People do change, priorities and lifestyles change. Family dynamics take their toll and family relationships are just what they are. My relationships with my sisters were waning. I had hoped that they would enjoy visiting the island and that it might be a way for us to be together again, like we used to when our mother lived here. It was not to be.

6 WHERE IT ALL HAPPENED

I made the move to Whidbey Island in 2011 - to find a quieter lifestyle and connect with the earth, attend to my health and my heart. I spent the past 15 years building a very successful business and it was time to begin closing that chapter of my life. I also lived the past 10 years a scant mile from the epicenter of the software giant Microsoft and its' main campus just down the street in Redmond, WA. The intensity of life that surrounds that campus can only be compared to the intensity of the advancements in technology over the past 20 years. Harried lives, impersonal interactions, constant heavy traffic on streets intended for a suburban lifestyle. I had no meaningful connection to the community, other than my business. Once a high school teacher in the community, I left that position in 1999 to begin my own business. My children were now grown and living on their own, so there were no longer the connections that happen between parents of band students or soccer players, or amongst neighbors with whose children your children played, etc. In defense of my neighbors, all lovely and many younger than I, a majority of my time and energy had been directed to the success of my business.

At this point in my life, the island was the perfect community for me. It felt "right" from the very beginning, and still does. I was perfectly content in my new/old 1930's craftsman bungalow located a block from the beach. I often walked down to the public section of the beach to sit and contemplate life, breathe in the fresh salty air and let my mind drift to a peaceful place. This beach is Columbia Beach and sits just south of and adjacent to the ferry dock where the ferry that brings both residents, tourists and commercial folks to and from the island docks each half hour. That ferry can be seen landing and leaving Clinton every half hour for 20 hours of each day. Columbia Beach faces east toward the Cascade mountain range and along the opposite shoreline sits the city of Everett and a US Navy homeport. On a clear day, one can stand on the beach and see snowcapped Mt. Baker to the north and majestic, "ice-cream cone" Mt. Rainier to the south. The body of water is Puget Sound and as one moves north it becomes Saratoga

Passage with Camano Island to the east, culminating in a narrow passage known as "Deception Pass" that leads to the wide-open Straits of Juan de Fuca . Deception Pass was named by the British explorer George Vancouver who believed the passage to be a calm bay and found it to be a deep and turbulent connection between the Straits of Juan de Fuca and Saratoga Passage and thus thought the waterway deceptive. Captain Vancouver also named the island after his lieutenant, Joseph Whidbey. Of course the largest island (Vancouver Island) was named after the captain.

The beach is a true Puget Sound beach - dark, coarse sand with vestiges of sea life interspersed. Empty shells are prevalent and can be found scattered and clustered as the shoreline wave action roughly places them daily up and down this beach known as Columbia. There is also an abundance of driftwood in all sizes and shapes. Driftwood in this case is composed of the remnants from two sources; 1. storms that over the years have eroded the coastline and undermined trees to the point that they collapse into the water and are set adrift and 2. Log booms (a floating corral of cut timber on its way to nearby lumber mills) that have broken apart during storms and set their cargo adrift to wash up on beaches up and down the Salish Sea.

There have been 3 major landslides on the south end of this shoreline since recording of such occurrences began mid-century. The waves and current never stop. They are constantly eroding, changing how the beach appears and what is to be found upon it. It is a lovely place to sit or walk. It should be noted that the state of Washington is one of the very few states in the U.S. where beaches can be owned by private individuals. Columbia Beach is a private beach, owned by those who own property on the shoreline. Many resident/owners are a little touchy about others having public access (especially tourists) and walking on "their" beach. Sigh. I mention this only to note that I did not feel comfortable sitting or walking on this beach, even though it was beautiful, and most often empty of any persons. That's why I usually sat on the small (about 150 feet long) public beach to the north side of the ferry dock.

When Joan mentioned the auction of the beach property, I was curious but not interested. As I thought about it over the next few days, curiosity did get the better of me and a few days later when my sister Katy was visiting, we set out to find the property. There in the middle of the yard was a large (4' x 5') sign announcing the upcoming public auction to be held right there at the property. I assumed it was a bank foreclosure and would find out later that many others believed the same. Given the economic times and real estate catastrophes of the past 4 years, it was a logical assumption.

To say the cottage was in disrepair would be an understatement. The paint was many years overdue for a new coat. The roof had a long dip like an old horse's back and the porches both appeared as if they were "falling off" the sides of the cottage. The separate garage to the left of the yard in the near corner was past the point of no return. The roof had caved in and a landslide some years before had filled it with dirt nearly half-way up the side walls. There was now a healthy covering of grass throughout the floor of the structure. Even using the term "floor" is a stretch of description because of the irregularity of the surface and all the debris that was scattered throughout. Behind the main garage was an attached shed that had locked doors. I fleetingly wondered what was inside. Were there antiques, any articles of value or hidden treasures? On the other side of the yard on the street side of the property was an old speedboat. It was a 1952 Skagit "plastic boat" in a faded pink and white, quite modern for its time, quite sad today. The windshield had hundreds of minute fractures in the plastic, making it impossible to see through. There were no motors on the back of the boat and all was covered by a thread-worn blue plastic tarp that flapped in the wind. The tarp no longer performed the job it was set there to do. The boat was taking in water and various forms of dirt, debris and green algae had been collecting and growing.

I walked between the collapsed garage and the boat onto the property and picked up a flyer from one of those plastic real estate boxes attached to a post. It turned out to be more of a written notice than a real estate information flyer. There were no photos, square footage, or listings of amenities, price, etc. The notice stated that there would be a "preview" or open house in one week - on a

Sunday afternoon and an auction the following week. The purpose of the open house was to allow possible buyers a view of the interior of the cottage, and an opportunity to meet the realtor and determine whether to return for the auction in one week. Little did I know that the door to the cottage was currently unlocked and had been unlocked for years. It seemed that the local neighbors all knew this as did some unknown individuals who walked off with several items from inside the cottage. I came by that information after the cottage was legally mine. I could have walked through the cottage on the day I first saw it, but I never would have, even if I had known.

Cottage just after auction in April 2012

7   A COTTAGE FOR SALE

The Preview

My neighbor, Mike, a retired architect with a very good eye for structures lives across the street from me. On the day of the open house I knocked on his door and asked if he would like to walk down to the cottage and take a look with me. He said "sure!" We set out walking down to the old cottage on the street below, about a 10 minute walk. The stairs into the cottage were structurally unsound and a safety liability. Downright scary! I was afraid that the rest of the cottage would be the same. As we went inside it was as if we were walking back nearly 90 years in time. The cottage appeared most likely just as it had for 87 years, ever since its construction in 1925.

My first observation was that it was very dark and dingy. Every room was filled with furniture, lamps, curtains, miscellaneous objects - fishing rods, a rolled-up sail from a boat, a wind sock and a few framed prints on the walls, magazines on small tables, etc. It looked lived in. The windows were covered with a heavy fabric in a jungle floral print of black, green and yellow. The draperies were worn, torn and faded with time and use, their once white lining now brown and stained. This darkened the rooms, adding to the dreariness and worn-out feeling that pervaded the cottage. Each room had a different patterned flooring on the floor, some geometric art deco, some with very native southwest designs, similar to the blankets you could buy on Native American reservations and typical of the 1940's. Atop the brown patterned living room flooring was a piece of gold shag carpeting that covered most of the floor. The rest of the rooms had only the linoleum-like flooring on the floor.

The front bedroom walls and ceiling were covered with a green on white floral print wallpaper. Water stains covered most of the wallpapered ceiling and walls where the roof had leaked over time. There were old mattresses on their side in this room and a 1950's era dressing table with a very large round mirror. I remember fishing rods and equipment being scattered about that bedroom and it looked very full, cluttered and tired.

Front bedroom

The only other parts of the house I remember were the bathroom, painted a sunny yellow, although the color was tinged with darkness from time. It had a dingy bathtub under an awning window and sitting in the very middle of the tub were a pair of very large, black rubber wading boots a fisherman would wear in a storm. An old, stained toilet leaned to one side on my right and sat facing a small sink that hung on the wall with a bucket (near overflowing) below, actively catching water from a leaky pipe. The floor sagged as I stepped onto it. Yikes!

Bathroom with bucket to catch leaking sink pipes

I remember so well that my neighbor Mike called it "charming" and after that comment we both agreed it was a big mess! It was well beyond what either of us wanted to tackle. It was probably a "scraper" - fit for tearing down and putting up a mega-house, maximizing every available square foot of the lot as the neighbors on both sides of the cottage had already done. The practice of "scraping" the old fishing cabins or cottages off and replacing with over-sized multistory homes was becoming the practice of beach property here and also along many of the beaches found in Puget Sound. I suppose it is a sign of prosperity and the changing times.

We spoke to the realtor, asked polite questions, learned that the property and all its contents were being sold "as is" and that the property would not pass inspection. That is realtor talk for "cash sale only". The septic, the foundation, the wiring, the porches the floors all would not pass a bank-ordered inspection. A bank would not consider it a good investment of their money and therefore would not grant a loan. If I had entertained any thoughts of buying, and I don't think I truly was, this information confirmed it. No way was I going to even think of buying, investing, etc.

Reason For the Sale

We also learned that it was not a distress sale or foreclosure but an auction to make the sale faster and easier. The owner, Wil, had fallen sometime in the previous months, hit his head and was taken to the local hospital near his home south of Seattle. The hospital could not locate his next of kin and thus Wil became a ward of the state. He lived alone at that time, his wife Lucille having died some 10 years earlier. Wil's step-daughter, Maridel and her husband lived most of the year in Mexico and could not be located. I do believe that they were not frequently in contact with Wil at this point in time. Maridel was never particularly close to Wil and since the death of her mother, Lucille, that relationship was mostly distant.

As I understand, becoming a ward of the state comes with the assignment of a guardian who will assist in making financial decisions among other tasks to help insure the welfare of the individual. Wil's guardian had already facilitated the sale of his home in Seattle and now was facilitating the sale of his fishing cottage on Whidbey Island. I suppose the proceeds go to the state to pay for his care in a state-operated facility. The guardian did not want the sale of the two properties to be a long, drawn out process consisting of the listing, multiple showings and the sale, thus electing to sell both homes at auctions. To the best of my knowledge, Wil was out of the hospital and living in an assisted care facility at the time of the auction. He was 88 years old.

Mike and I left the cottage "open house" and talked about it as we walked back up the hill to our homes on the street above the cottage. We agreed that it was "charming" and that at some time in its history it must have been a very cute cottage. That was all. Out of mind - or so I thought.

The Auction

The following Saturday arrived. I probably thought once or twice about the cottage, wondering who would buy it and curious what an auction was like, but that was all. At 11:40am on the morning of the scheduled auction, it was raining. The skies were dark and overcast and the temperature was chilly in the upper 40's. The auction was set for noon. I sat in my chair that morning, looking out over the water. I have a small peek-a-boo eastern view of the water and the Cascade mountains, both were barely visible on this rainy, foggy morning. Something, I'm not sure if it was curiosity or fate, caused me to put my coat on, grab an umbrella, put the leash on my dog and head out the door. I stopped a small distance from the house and decided that having Chester (my dog) with me would be difficult, so I brought him back to the house and then headed down to the cottage, a 10 minute walk.

I arrived at the cottage at 11:55am, about 5 minutes before the auction. I shook off my umbrella and leaned it against the outside of the cottage. The stairs were not in good condition and slanted seriously. On the face of one riser was a metal sign stating "NO ADMITTANCE". I wonder how many people had ignored that sign over the years.

As I entered the front door into the small living room I felt the presence of several people standing around. Immediately across from the doorway sat my friend Joan. She waved, said "Hi Sue!" and introduced me to her elderly neighbor sitting beside her who was hooked up to a personal oxygen tank. Remember Joan is 85 as are many of the long-time residents of this beach community. There is a great culture alive and well on that beach (I had yet to understand this). There are the "long-timers" who have lived there 50+ years; the relatives of the long-timers; the inheritors of the property passed down from long-timers; and the newcomers.

I walked into the living room, now a bit brighter with the curtains opened up, and found the realtor around the corner in the kitchen. He had placed his forms and documents on the kitchen table - one of those dinette sets from the 1950's with aluminum legs and grey patterned Formica tabletop. The realtor/auctioneer a tall slender man in his late 50's stated that if I intended to bid, I had to register. I asked whether you had to bid if you registered and he said "no." So I pulled out one of the chrome chairs and sat down on the grey "marble print" vinyl upholstery to fill out the necessary paper for "registering".

The scene of the auction - the living room

The realtor gave me my auction number and I returned to the living room to sit on the end of the floral, autumn-colored Herculon hide-a-bed couch. Joan was sitting right across from me, smiling like a Cheshire cat.

The room was filled with people - standing and sitting wherever possible. I thought to myself that this was going to be an interesting auction. One should understand that I have never been to an auction, let alone ever participated in an auction with such high stakes. I had no idea what I was going to observe but everyone seemed excited. I was there (or so I told myself) to observe an auction. Just another curious cat. I believed it would be very interesting. I also wanted to know what sort of a price this cottage would actually sell for. I'd heard rumors that auctions can be places where you can get a "steal" of a buy. This was yet to be discovered. The auctioneer (realtor) put on his headset with microphone attached to a speaker. Mind you, this was a 10' x 14' room, hardly large enough to need a loudspeaker and everyone was certainly quiet enough to hear even a whisper. I suppose there is a sense of auctioneer professionalism conveyed by the microphone and headset.

We all became quiet and the realtor began the auction, as one would expect from movies and such, it did start with "do I hear an opening bid of $50,000?" He said it again, "do I hear an opening bid of $50,000?" Once again, everyone there looked at everyone else. Was anybody going to bid? I had expected a competitive bidding war. I have since learned that the folks there wanted to be at the auction for a variety of reasons: 1. Watch it go for big money so their property values would escalate, 2. Buy it themselves at a "steal", 3. Buy it for a friend/relative, 4. Find a prospective buyer for their own property currently for sale (as one neighbor was actually doing) or 5. Witness the sale, whatever the outcome, to satisfy curiosity and say "I was there." The curious "looky-loos". I fall into the latter category - I was just plain curious.

We sat there, silently, with the tangible feel of a tingly, expectant tension in the room, waiting for someone to say something. From around the corner, in the kitchen and out of sight, a man stated

"$50,000". That was the beginning. I waited to see if someone would counter-offer, no one did. The auctioneer was asking "do I hear $60,000?" Not a single response in the whole room of people - amazing! I thought to myself, and this was the first time my mind even went there, "well I can find $60,000"! Imagine - moving from not even thinking, at least on a conscious level, about buying the property to thinking "I can do this!" What a leap that was. I believe I was caught up in the excitement of the auction - I understand people do get caught up in the excitement, spurred on by the competition and end up with something they didn't need or end up offering a price they really cannot afford.

Now I was engaged and something within me, that competitive spirit "thing" rose up and took over. I was on the edge of my seat, listening to the back and forth and as I listened, I heard my own voice - I was bidding! The amazing thing - there was only one other bidder! All those people filling the cottage and just two of us bidding. I had no idea what I was doing - remember I have never done this before. At one point, I out-bid myself. The auctioneer politely told me "you already have the high bid." Oh. OK - I had a quirky smile and laughed at myself. Good grief! After several minutes of bidding back and forth, we arrived at $150,000 - the man around the corner and myself. I had the high bid. The auctioneer asked for $160,000. No response. He asked for $155,000. No response. He asked for $151,000. NO RESPONSE! I might have just bought myself a beach cottage! We all sat there in suspended silence. I was so nervous, I did not hear a thing going on around me until he said, "SOLD for $150,000!" I just sat there. All I heard was a pulsating in my ears and my heart pounding . I was exhilarated and panic-stricken. What have I done? WHAT HAVE I DONE!

I know people said things to me, I truly did not hear them. At some point, and it must have been when the realtor asked me to come into the kitchen, I stood up and moved back to the kitchen table. He said "congratulations" and I told him that I was so nervous that I was shaking. He said, "don't get too nervous, the deal is not done yet." What? Not done? What does that mean? The realtor proceeded to explain that the guardian had to "approve" the sale and that she could counter offer. I was surprised and thought that was a curious version of an auction. My experience (with movies and television at least) told me that when the gavel came down and the auctioneer said "sold", it meant just that. Not so today.

I sat there with my stomach doing flip-flops and I was thinking "where the heck am I going to find $150,000!? I mean really - where? I was so caught up in the excitement of winning the auction, I hadn't given this any thought! I'm not an irresponsible person. Everything I have done in my life has been very well thought out. I always do research, check my heart and my bank account, weigh the pros and cons, read my horoscope (not really), before I make big decisions or purchases. I had done none of that on this HUGE decision and purchase. My heart was pounding, palms sweaty and I couldn't actually think of what I needed to ask this realtor before I left the auction. I did write a check - earnest money. In hindsight, there were so many questions I could have, should have asked.

Instead, he spoke to me and let me know the basics of what had just transpired. I would not be able to get a loan because the structure did not/would not pass inspection. (It was in pretty bad shape). He would take the offer to his client, the owner's court-appointed guardian and we would hear in a few days whether the offer was accepted. He also let me know that the guardian might counter-offer and in that case, I could accept or decline.

As I headed toward the front door to leave, several folks (turns out that they were all neighbors) came up to me and offered congratulations. Several gave their thoughts on what they thought was going to happen verses what just did happen. The neighbor to the north, Jim, stopped me to talk about his house that was for sale next door. He pointed out a sign that had been placed on the side of his house that morning, facing the front door to the cottage. I suppose he put it there on that specific day to attract a potential buyer for his home. As he continued to talk, he explained that perhaps someone would want to buy the cottage for the land and buy his house also, thus giving the buyer a double lot and room to expand. I have no idea what folks thought of me in that room.

None knew me - they might have thought I was some Microsoft millionaire with tons of money, ready to bulldoze the property (or to buy the property next door), it didn't work out that way. Jim and his wife Diane have since sold their house and moved to eastern Washington.

The Aftermath

I left the cottage with a handful of signed documents (my signatures and the realtor signatures), inflated my umbrella and walked home. I was both excited and nervous, I don't think I was scared. I knew that if I could not raise the money, I would forfeit the earnest money but nothing else. I also knew that the guardian could counter-offer and I could refuse. That was not the route I wanted to take, but it was an option. Before I went into my house I stopped by Mike's house and simply said "I bought it!" He jumped up and asked me to repeat my statement and then said "you are kidding!?" Nope, not kidding. I called both of my sisters, they were not excited. I think they were puzzled. Maybe they had some other emotion - a beach cottage for $150,000 was an incredible deal. My brother-in-law was excited, he said, "great, now you can hire me to come up there and fix it up!" A different sort of excitement than I had. I called my cousin and she was excited and asked a ton of questions. In the end, she was the one who dedicated much time and energy to help me renovate the cottage. I did also hire contractors and my two neighbors, Mike an architect (retired) and his brother Dan a structural engineer (retired) who worked extensively and flawlessly on everything from replacing damaged flooring in 3 rooms to painting the exterior of the cottage.

That evening, I received a call from a neighbor of the cottage, two doors down to the north. Her name is Toot and she along with her husband LeeRoy, also known as Roy, became the most helpful, joyful friends I would meet on the beach. Their knowledge of the beach, the history, the politics, the maintenance issues as well as their friendship were such a blessing to me. Toot called to introduce herself to me and to let me know that if there was anything I needed, to not hesitate to come knock on their door or give them a call. I did just that, many, many times.

The next morning was April 1, April Fools' Day. What a day to think through what had just transpired - what I had just done. Last night I dreamed about the cottage and in my dream it was called the "Creamsicle Cottage" - painted Creamsicle orange, white trim with aqua windows and door, surrounded by flowers and a white picket fence. That was the vision I consistently saw when I thought of the beach cottage. It was a long way from the very sad, run-down fishing cottage I had just successfully bid on in an auction. I am a planner, dreamer and doer - so my thinking went into overdrive. Isn't it wonderful when a big project falls in your lap? A project that involves creativity, vision, planning, shopping, working and bringing a dream into reality. I know that I do love those activities and I was excited.

I spent about 45 minutes total in the cottage - I didn't even walk through it after I won the auction. I still did not know if it would be mine. The guardian could come back with a refusal of the offer or a counter-offer that was well beyond my reach. I was scrambling to think of where I was going to come up with $150,000 cash. If it was much more money than that, I don't know how I would be able to make that happen.

A few days later, I received a phone call from the realtor. The guardian had refused my offer. My heart sank. She had countered with a new amount of $200,000. I had to think. Yes, it was still a ridiculously low price to pay for a slice of the beach. Yes, the cottage would need at least $100,000 in cleaning-up, (turned out to be more - of course), landfill costs, renovation and a lot of hard work. That means I would have to come up with about $300,000 in cash. One thing to know about me (amongst many things you will soon know) is that I do not "haggle" on price. My kids always roll their eyes when I am in Mexico at a flea market and pay full price for some object or piece of jewelry. I figure people ask for the price they need. OK - there is also the fact that I don't like conflict. So I did not come back with my own counter-offer as I know I could have. It still was a great purchase price and I feel good about it. At some level, there was a person at the other end of the financial deal.

In my decision-making data file were the contextual factors of my life. I am a single person, living modestly in a home built in the 1930's (that I love). I was a school teacher for 27 years before starting my own business 15 years ago. In that business, seven of those years were not profitable and the past eight years have been profitable to varying degrees. I raised two children as a single parent. I have very intentionally contributed to my retirement fund for my whole career. The decisions I was now dealing with were do I tap into those funds to buy a beach cottage? Do I take out a second mortgage on my primary home? Do I empty my savings account? This was a difficult decision for a single person at age 63 years who would soon be retiring. These thoughts and more pinged back and forth in my mind for several days.

The day after the auction I happened to be going to LaConner, a quaint waterfront town north east of Whidbey Island, to meet two good friends for Sunday breakfast. We talked about the opportunity and all the implications. They said, "if nothing else, it is a great investment, go for it!" My neighbor Mike said, "if I had the money I would do it." My cousin said, "I'll loan you money if you need some." My business partner said "if you don't want it, let me know because I want to buy it." Very different directives and reasons, all of them pointing me to my decision: Yes, I will buy it!

I did accept the counter-offer of $200k. With the real estate transaction done, I was given 60 days to come up with $200,000 cash. Considering the number of transactions and applications I had to accomplish in that time, that amount of time was none too long. In the end I took out a home equity loan, a loan from my 401k and emptied my savings account and liquidated some cash investment accounts. I managed to get it all done on time and handed the Title Company a check for $200,000 on June 7, 2012. A done deal, for better or for worse. In the title documents was a photocopy of the deed showing Berte Olson signing ownership over to Wilbur for paying off a note in 1958 that was created when he purchased the cottage from Berte's sister in 1954. It did not mean much to me at the time. That would change.

The beach cottage was mine. I felt like celebrating - with someone!

It was just another quiet day in my house. There are quite a few of those quiet days, where the only conversations I have are with my dogs or on the telephone. I work at home most days, so phone calls are the norm. Actual people in my house are not the norm. I often think about that. The increasing feeling of loneliness or being alone. I realize that loneliness and being alone are two very different feelings and states of being. One can be alone without being lonely and one can be surrounded by people and be lonely. More and more I have been thinking about the difference between being alone and being lonely and what does it mean to me? The upcoming journey with the Creamsicle Cottage would teach me a lot about loneliness and being alone.

Author's first visit back to the cottage after auction

8 STEPPING BACK IN TIME

I didn't celebrate the formal possession of the beach cottage, but I was very excited! The planning became very real and a lot of fun. My mind was in hyper drive thinking of all the possibilities. The challenges and opportunities, are what it all comes down to. There were challenges to be overcome, and problems to solve, and soon I would find out how many. There were so many opportunities to step into, actually many more than I thought for.

My first visit into the cottage after the sale was with my son Bryan. I wanted him to document what I found and the original condition of the structure and contents. This was the first time I really had an opportunity to explore what the cottage was and what it contained. I had much to learn about it and its charming history. Both doors were unlocked, one of them would not lock. This is when I learned that it had been unlocked for years. Many of the neighbors knew this and from time-to-time walked through it out of curiosity and, perhaps, other motivations.

I stepped into the cottage, through the same door I entered just before the auction. It was like visiting the scene of something big after all the participants have gone home. It was quiet with the murmur of the auctioneer faintly alive in the background. I looked around at the chairs where the "looky-loos" had been sitting, now empty. The door I entered leads directly into the living room. I could really see, for the first time, the cottage and what it actually contained. I was no longer looking through emotional eyes or through a room full of people. It was dark as the curtains were pulled over the windows. I noticed immediately that the room had a chemical smell that I assume was due to the oil heater that sat right in the midst of the living room. When I removed the heater during the initial clean-out, the smell was no longer present.

Oil heater in living room

I was surprised and very pleased that there was no mildew or mold nor any lingering dampness or smell from the dampness. As it turned out, there was no mildew anywhere in, on or under the cottage. Aside from the stained wallpaper in one of the bedroom ceilings from a leaky roof, there was no water damage anywhere - that in itself was remarkable for a house existing in a cold and damp climate on the beach. The curtains were a very dark print, popular in the 1950's. They were now threadbare and torn. On one of the tables sat a lamp fashioned out of a piece of burled driftwood, its shade dusty and sooty from time and the oil heating. The oil heater sat prominently in the living room against the far wall. It was rather large, about 4 feet high, 2 feet wide and 2 feet deep fashioned in a dark metal with a flue-stack rising out the top, making a 90 degree turn and disappearing into the wall. The sofa was a floral print Herculon fabric in gold tones and the two swivel rockers were upholstered in gold velvet. In one corner of the room stood a tall, narrow table with a few books and Popular Mechanics magazines on the shelves. The floor was covered with a brown and gold shag carpeting that was just laying on top of old asbestos linoleum in a brown Native American blanket pattern. The linoleum had long ago separated from the floor and was just laying on top of the floor boards.

I moved through the living room into the kitchen. It was neat and clean although the sink was stained from a faucet that must have dripped for many years. The kitchen dinette table and chairs in tubular steel and grey Formica sat as it must have for over 50 years. A nice walk-in pantry accessed through a small door in the corner of the kitchen was filled with pots and pans, an old electric mixer (still in its box), and various other kitchen tools and equipment. A set of white painted tin canisters adorned with blue flowers and topped with yellow lids were filled with flour, sugar and tea bags.

There was also a case of toothpick boxes - a whole case of the round wood toothpicks. Perhaps Wil built models from them? The small linoleum counter sat empty. The linoleum pattern was an off-white color with streaks of red and grey. The edge of the counter was framed with a metal stripping that had red rubber embedded in the center of the stripping. The two small shelves just above the counter held small glass serving pieces and a little honey pot.

The cabinet above the counter held all the dishes, serving plates, mugs and glasses. On the very top shelf there was an extensive collection of salt and pepper shakers undoubtedly collected from many vacation adventures to National Parks, beach towns, mountain curio shops and antique shops. I'm sure some were gifts. What a precious collection.

I opened the door between the kitchen and the back porch. This door was the original outside back door and became an inside door when the porch was framed in and made weather tight. Black rubber storm gear - hat, pants and jacket were hanging on hooks over the windows inside the porch where Wil must have hung them after his last repair venture, perhaps shoring up the bulkhead or replacing shingles on the roof. The enclosed porch housed the water heater and the electric fuse panel. Electricity was knob and tube and there were spare fuses sitting atop the panel.

Back porch with storm gear

At the end of the 5 x 8 porch a bathroom had been added. This was probably done when the cottage was brought down to south Whidbey and set on Columbia Beach from its original home on Fidalgo Island. The original cottage had neither indoor plumbing or hot water so both the bathroom and the water heater were additions. There was a small sink mounted onto the left wall of the bathroom and a bucket under the sink was full. I emptied it into the bathtub and replaced it under the sink. It would continue to fill up with the dripping from the cold water faucet until I had the plumbing repaired. I looked into the vanity mirror on the front of a metal vanity cabinet above the sink. The mirror was losing its reflective layer around the edges. Inside on rusty shelving were small cardboard boxes of bandages and an empty metal "Bandaid" box with a flip top. Not much more.

In the master bedroom, there was a double bed, neatly made with a threadbare, white chenille bedspread. A nightstand sat at the far edge of the bed and contained several magazines from the 1950's, mostly Popular Mechanics and Mechanix Illustrated.

The only other piece of furniture in the room was a tall bureau or dresser with a small round mirror mounted on top. The rounded edges and blond veneer of the dresser was very popular in the 1950's. It's mate was in the other bedroom, a dressing table with a 40" diameter mirror mounted on the top.

Inside the tall bureau were drawers lined in newspaper. In those drawers were clean, very neatly folded items. One drawer was filled with bedroom sheets in various patterns and colors from yellow and orange flowers to blue and green plaid. Another drawer was filled with kitchen linens. Some of those were lovely kitchen towels made of dishcloth cotton, soft from many years of use and embroidered with the day of the week and a scene. Monday's towel has a girl baking pies and so on. Some of the towels were orange and green printed terrycloth and quite worn. Two special towels of the era had a cotton fabric/button end that could be inserted and buttoned over the handle of the stove. They were gold, orange and green terrycloth towels. These remain in the cottage today and remind me vividly of a tender time in the life of a quiet man and his wife. He or they wasted nothing. Many other towels had multiple holes in them and were relegated to a paper bag and probably saved for "rags".

In another drawer were the carefully folded remnants of his wife's clothing. His wife Lucille died 10 years before. An ivory knit sweater, a bathing suit, a bathing cap and a printed silk scarf plus a few other items. Why that particular collection of his wife's clothing remained is a mystery to me.

The top drawer contained various miscellaneous items. Old tide tables going back to the 1950's, tools, pencils and small note pads. Sort of what I would call a "junk drawer".

On the floor of the small closet at the back of this bedroom sat an Electrolux vacuum cleaner, still in its original box. On the top shelf of the closet was a badminton set and 4 dusty cardboard boxes, about 3" thick and 10" x 14" wide and tall. The sides were printed in various one-color designs and on the top of each was a clear cellophane panel, allowing the contents to be viewed. These were original display boxes for 4 different dolls.

"The Dolls of All Nations" - collectables from the Duchess Doll Corporation, manufactured in the 1940's and 50's. Original cost was $1.95/doll (my cousin looked them up on the Internet). The 4 dolls represent Italy, France, Spain and Germany and were likely not taken out of their boxes very often as they are in perfect shape. The eyes still blink when you tip the dolls back and forth. I imagine they belonged to Maridel, Wil's step-daughter.

The other bedroom, to the right of the front door, was added when the cottage was brought down to Columbia Beach. It has two windows and the walls were the only walls in the cottage covered with wallpaper. As I would find out later, they were constructed of rough-hewn 4" cedar planking on the horizontal. The rest of the main cottage walls are constructed of bead board mounted horizontally. As I mentioned earlier, the walls and ceiling of this bedroom were water-stained and the room was filled with old beds on their sides, folding chairs, fishing net, fishing rods, a torn sail from a small sailboat or catamaran and other various large items in storage. This room along with the living room were the most depressing rooms for me to be in and think about how I would be able to clean up and transform them. This bedroom addition has an actual door to the living room in contrast to the original bedroom that has a doorway with a wooden rod mounted above for a privacy curtain.

As I left the bedrooms and moved back out into the living room I felt compelled to stop and take down the curtains. The darkness of the room was stifling. The difference when I removed both sets of curtains was remarkable, there was hope! And feeling better, I walked into the kitchen. It was painted in a soft yellow, also very typical of the 1950's. The single wall cabinet was made of bead board with glass fronts. The stove and refrigerator were not 1950 era but rather 1980 or so? Both were still working and in fair condition. Gingerly I opened the refrigerator door - there was food inside. I was surprised to see an apple and a few other perishables not covered in mold or totally shriveled up. Someone must have left them there in the recent month, I was not sure who it might have been. There were also the usual condiments like ketchup, pickle relish and mustard. The freezer had some vegetable relics.

On top of the refrigerator sat a tide clock - battery run and capable of displaying high and low tides. I didn't understand then how significant it would be to someone living on the beach. Beside it was a barometer and temperature gauge, something often displayed by those living near the water. I was overwhelmed by the volume of "stuff" I had to deal with. In the end, I threw a lot of "stuff" out. I might have saved it and dealt with an antique dealer, but at the time, I could not imagine taking it all out and saving it somewhere to be dealt with later. It was beyond my energy level and what I wanted to mentally handle.

Out in the shed, which only had the resemblance of a lock on the door, was a collection of old yard tools and implements. Most were rusted beyond saving. There also sat two (55) gallon steel drums, one was connected by copper tubing to the oil burner in the living room. This was the source of fuel for heating the cottage. There were also several boat oars of various sizes and colors and a rusted gas can. On the "garage side" of this building were several anodized bolts of a very large nature. I came to learn that Wil was a lineman for a telephone company and the garage contained several items that he probably came into possession of while working. They could have been extra bolts or retired bolts and the wood cross-members through which the telephone lines were strung. I kept the wood cross-members and gave away the bolts.

At the front of the garage facing the street was mounted a carved wooden address plate with the house number and Wil's last name. It read "The Mills 6627". My last name is Mills. This would not be the first occasion for me to consider the destiny of this cottage and how it came to be in my possession. Stated in another way, I was (possibly) destined to own this cottage. Now that is quite a statement, but I could not deny that the plaque on the outside of the house with the same name was making me think about it. At this writing, the plaque still resides on the front of the house.

Throughout this first adventure into my new cottage, Bryan took a complete set of photographs, documenting the condition and contents of the cottage. The memory can dim and fade, but a photo has the ability to capture the reality of the moment.

9 THE PERSONAL LENS

A month after my accepted offer of $200,000, and before the sale was final, my sisters, their spouses, my son and daughter, son-in-law and his mother came up to enjoy a combination Easter and Mother's Day supper at my home. It was a lovely day in late April. Temperatures in the high 60's with sunshine, blue skies and a warm breeze. Spring was in full bloom, the daffodils in front of my house had all bloomed the week before. The grass was lush and green. Summer seemed to be just around the corner. We finished a late lunch - scheduled so that my family could catch a ferry on each side without having to wait in a long ferry line.

Ahhh, the ferry line - incredibly irritating to some and to others it seems to be just part of living on or visiting Whidbey. The ferry is one of those factors that simply "is" and all the grumbling won't change anything except perhaps your mood. My family and I don't get together very much at my house anymore and I know that the ferry line plays a part in that. In addition, busy lives and family dynamics are factors. Life is always interesting in families. It seems the longer we live, the more opportunity for relationship challenges. My family is no different.

After our meal was over, we walked down to the cottage. My family had not seen it, not even photos, and I was excited to show them. This was the first group of people with whom I was sharing this daring decision and adventure. It felt like I was getting ready to set out on a journey to an unknown territory. In my heart-of-heart I knew it was the right thing, but that still didn't prevent all the "what if's" from blazing a path through my calmness, leaving thoughts of have I made a big mistake? or how will I possibly make my way through this all alone? I was wanting support and excitement and just possibly offers of I'd love to help! That didn't happen. If anyone felt excited or supportive, they did not express it. That day, only negatives were spoken.

As we approached the cottage from the street, the sagging roof, collapsing garage, old speedboat in the yard, house paint peeling and the unsafe stairways leading inside caught the attention of most people there. Opening the door and stepping inside the first sight included the ugly, brown metal oil burner. It was surrounded by the old, dated furniture and thread-bare, shag rug on the floor. A water-damaged ceiling and stained wallpaper in the front bedroom as well as all the old stuff (beds on their sides, fishing equipment, coolers, lawn furniture, boxes containing unknown contents, etc.) piled about in the bedroom and added to the overall impression. Venturing further into the cottage, the water corrosion stains in the kitchen sink, the dingy bathtub and the bucket on the bathroom floor over-brimming with water from a leaky sink added insult to injury for the old wooden cottage. I do understand how that must have looked to them and yet I was still hoping for some level of congratulations or excitement.

The group left the cottage shortly after entering it. It is after all, only 660 square feet in size. We walked out to the massive amounts of driftwood between the edge of the cottage lawn and the open sand of the beach. This driftwood at the edge of the beach is different than most people anticipate when they think of a beach and my family was no exception. There was immediate talk of bringing trucks and machinery onto the beach and hauling it away. I am sure they were expecting a sand beach up to the lawn as this beach had been at one time. In 2003 a massive landslide and storm moved all those logs out into the water a few miles south of the cottage and deposited them on this beach. Those logs, now driftwood still remain in 2012, and have become old and grey in various stages of decomposition some nine years later. In not so many years, the logs will disappear and the sand will return to restore the beach and allow it to meet beachfront expectations.

We picked our way over the gigantic logs, roots and miscellaneous weather-beaten wood that had amassed on the beach and found a place to sit on a single gigantic log by the water. As we all sat there, looking back at the cottage in it's lonely and very worn state of disrepair, the conversation and comments again centered on the problems. The sagging roof, the broken stairs, the uneven floor, the assumptions that the foundation was probably rotted and/or insect infested. This talk was all rather disappointing to me. I had wanted and hoped for some sort of support or just maybe a statement or two about how fortunate I was to buy this cottage or how great it would be once it was fixed up. One of my brother-in-laws is a remodeling contractor (remember his initial excitement and his proclamation that I could hire him to fix it up)? He had no interest in fixing it up now. At one point amidst the dark haze of what was wrong with it, I declared "I like it and I think it is going to be a wonderful beach cottage." I felt very disconnected from them at that moment.

I had a very different vision of the old cottage. I thought then and I still believe that the age of the cottage is one of its most endearing factors. It was built in the 1920's, and it is 90 years old. I think that is fantastic. It also stood almost exactly as it was built 90 years ago. In many ways, it had been carefully preserved. I knew it had challenges, but I saw past the challenges and through to the treasure hidden underneath. I have learned that this is a gift of mine. I see the future, after transformation and I hold that vision until it is before me in reality. That is the essence of my dance with challenges - can I take them through to the vision I hold? How will I get through the obstacles that appear to be in my way? Many people would not have seen the beauty in the old cottage and would have torn it down and built something new. I went in just the opposite direction, I tried to preserve as much of the original structure and interior finishes as I could. I wanted the cottage to exist as it had in 1925.

I have come to realize that my family did not see what I saw because they were looking through the lens of their own life experiences. Members of your family of origin (in this case my sisters), even though you all grew up in the same household still view life through their own lens, tempered by their own experiences and because of that, often possess a viewpoint quite different from your own.

My children were looking through their own lens and most likely were wondering what impact this decision of mine would have on them. "What is mom doing?" Not a unique wondering. It does seem that many of my friends and colleagues in their 60's and approaching retirement or perhaps newly retired are making different decisions about their future than they have made in the past. Seeking peaceful places to experience "being" as opposed to the constant state of "doing". The past practice of seeking a safe and convenient place to raise a family and conduct a career is no longer the driving force behind real estate decisions. When my children were young, the priorities or deciding factors for where we would live had to do with schools, safety and the commute to work. When children leave home and you no longer work, the priorities change. My children were not used to my new priorities. I was also approaching the time in my financial life when I would be on a "fixed income". How I manage my resources is important to my children. I understand that and believe that my management of resources should not have a negative financial impact upon my children. I do my best to make wise decisions and stay financially healthy. I understand their reactions and still feel that this decision was a good one.

Most of my family members, now that the cottage is totally renovated, have openly proclaimed that it is wonderful and a real treasure. I suspect some of them would even proclaim that they always thought it was a good decision and were excited about it from the beginning. That is an example of the dance between perception and memory - something that fuels many, if not most of the dynamics amongst family members. We remember differently.

Multiple neighbors continually stop by to say how absolutely cute the cottage is and how glad they are that I did not destroy it. It is known as "the cutest cottage on the beach". My friends also think the same and enjoy the cottage, its sweet historical nature and the awesome quality of the coastline and beach that is the Salish Sea.

I find the dance of "family dynamics" which is grounded in the differences of our perceptions (and our memories) to be an interesting context of life. It continues to be an opportunity to grow in this lifetime and carries with it much frustration and sadness.

10 THE SOUL OF THE COTTAGE

Toward the end of the cottage restoration and behind my fierce desire to preserve this historical structure, I believe the spirits of the persons who previously owned the cottage had a definite influence on me. Did I hear them speak to me? That is to say did I actually hear spoken voices? No. Did I feel their presence and their energy? Yes I did. I most definitely felt the passion in which both of the previous owners held this cottage and what it meant to them. They have spoken to me in various ways ever since I walked away from the auction a winner and they continue to communicate with me and influence me.

Berte Olson loved the cottage and was a fierce, strong woman who with her husband in the 1920's owned and captained a ferry boat, something no other woman had done before. While she ran that business she lived in a cottage on Fidalgo Island, north of Whidbey Island and lived in it at that location for over 10 years. In 1936 her husband left her and her business on Whidbey ended. Berte loaded all her contents into her cottage, barged it to her new work site on Hood Canal where she began a new business and raised her children. In 1940 she barged a cottage down to Whidbey Island and set it upon a new foundation on Columbia Beach for her sister to live in for over 10 years. It is not known whether this was her original cottage that had been previously barged to Hood Canal or if it was another one.

Wil and his wife bought the cottage in 1954. He called it "my fishing cottage". He dearly loved it. It meant escape from work, provided quiet time, fishing experiences and wonderful time spent with his wife. For he and his wife, the longest stays in the cottage were a week to two weeks in length. It was truly a fishing cottage for him, not insulated, quite drafty and cold in the winter. The oil heater must have kept the living room quite warm, but the other rooms had no source of heat. As such, whenever he and his wife left for the season, he drained all the water pipes and the water heater. I do not know if he kept the oil heater on at a minimum. When Berte's sister lived in the cottage from 1940-54, a fully-heated cabin was a luxury. Occupants piled on the quilts, heated a rock or a brick, wrapped it in a towel and took it to bed with them. Previous to its journey down to Columbia Beach, the only source of heat was a wood-burning kitchen stove. We won't accept that level of discomfort or inconvenience any more. The cottage speaks to me of a simpler life where there is not so much to take care of and you are in touch with the essence of life because you are not buffered from it by layers of things. Life can be wonderful even without all the luxuries or the size and comforts of a big, fancy house.

The Original Cottage

Several changes/improvements were made when the cottage was brought down to Whidbey Island for Berte's sister. A covered porch accessed through the original backdoor from the kitchen was added. It contained a bathroom and also housed the water heater and electrical fuse panel which may or may not have been there previously. I do not believe running water/plumbing existed in the original cottage. I'm not sure about the electricity. The wiring was knob and tube and was in very good condition throughout the cottage. That same wall between the kitchen and the porch also has a wood box. On the outside wall is a 2x2x3 box with a hinged lid and on the kitchen side next to the original back door is an opening in the wall with a drop-down door. This is where wood could be stored and accessed without going out into the cold. A 2nd bedroom was added on the west end of the living room when the cottage was brought down to Whidbey Island. This bedroom has the luxury of a wooden door offering it more privacy than the original bedroom had although the original bedroom did have a small 3' closet space in the corner, something the new bedroom didn't have.

The entire interior of the cottage was finished in old-growth fir and cedar. The walls and ceilings were bead board, the floors were 3" wood planks and the trim was fir and cedar. All wood had darkened through the years and was the reddish-brown color of a dark cedar chest. If it was ever varnished, very little varnish still existed. The window trim throughout the house had never been painted and had that dark reddish-brown color. The living room had been painted a fleshy beige. The kitchen and bathroom were both painted a light, sunny yellow. The main bedroom was painted a very light lilac color while the 2nd bedroom was covered with wallpaper. The covered porch was painted the original grey of the exterior of the cottage.

The exterior of the cottage as I found it in 2012 was a very weathered light grey with many areas having flaked off to expose the raw wood underneath. The current window casings, trim and doors on the outside of the cottage were painted a turquoise green or aqua green. I discovered when I refinished the windows that years ago they were painted red. The original cottage was probably a light grey or white with red trim.

An old brick chimney stuck out of the center of the cottage roof and on top of that was a metal chimney extension, slightly listing to one side. The roof was a study in extremes - one half was in desperate need of repair and the other half looked just fine. I was to learn that one half had been reroofed recently with a composition shingle, somewhere in the past 10 years and the other half had original cedar shingles. I would also learn that Wil used to go up onto the roof when he was in his 70's and early 80's with a few shingles under his arm and replace missing shingles, one-by-one.

The bottom 2' below the siding of the house was a skirt made of several rows of cedar shingles and covered the portion between the ground and the elevated bottom of the house. I could not see beyond that skirt to view what was under the house. It is probably a good thing as it was a mess and I might have been overwhelmed at that point in discovery. Wil had gone under the house on more than one occasion and using multiple jacks he had lifted or elevated various portions of the cottage. Two forces had worked against the level nature of the cottage: 1. The decomposing driftwood that had been buried by sand over time and upon which the cottage was placed and 2. In 1996 a landslide from the hillside behind the cottage slid into the cottage along with a tree it was pushing and moved the cottage 5-8" from its original placement in places. That meant that the posts were no longer standing at a 90 degree angle (or perpendicular) to the beams they were supporting and the cottage was nearly falling over. There were at least 8 jacks in various places under the cottage floor. My vision of Wil crawling under the cottage and placing those jacks is scary. On top of the work he was doing under the house in a 20" crawlspace, he was 6'3" and in his 70's and 80's.

History of the Area

Those are the first impressions I had of the cottage and its owners. Since that time I have come to know much more about each of them. As I stated earlier, I learned about Berte through historical documents and books and through Jill Johnson the story teller who did research to discover all she could about Berte. I learned about Wil from neighbors and from his journals.

Wil was a utilities lineman who worked on maintaining and repairing telephone lines and often worked overtime to repair downed lines when a storm went through. He had no children of his own. His wife had one child. They owned a house in Kent, their primary residence and the cabin they called a fishing cottage. Most of the beach cottages that sprang up in the 20's through the 40's were fishing cottages or cabins. Several fishing resorts also appeared during that time on the various beaches around Whidbey Island. Only a handful of those resorts still exist and most have been sold off the small cabins, one-by-one to individuals for their beach cabins. In time those individual cabins have been renovated or totally rebuilt after demolition and their genesis as one of several resort cabins cannot be detected. There were two such resorts on Columbia Beach, tiny light green cottages can be seen clustered together close to the ferry. The other, known as "Jim 'n' Johns" is gone. Berte's cottage was placed nearly at the end of the road - Columbia Beach Road in the 1940's. There were 2 or 3 cabins beyond it and there the road ended. Beyond the road was an estuary surrounding a run-off and it was at this estuary that a tribal chief and a small band of Native Americans from the Skykomish tribe would camp for several weeks in the summer. During that time they would fish, clam and crab and dry their bounty of the sea so it would last throughout the winter months. At the end of summer they would canoe back to their home across the big water known as the Salish Sea. To those who have not heard of the Salish Sea, it is Puget Sound and I am referring to the stretch called Saratoga Passage, the passage between Whidbey Island and the mainland from Mukilteo to well above Everett. My friend and neighbor Roy Young would venture down there as a young man (unbeknownst to his parents) in the late 1930's to early 40's and spend time with the chief and his tribal members sitting around the fire and listening to stories. The chief presented Roy with a hand-carved canoe paddle at the end of one summer. It still sits above his fireplace.

With the extension of the road and the additional 40 beach cabins built along that road, the estuary disappeared. Gone also is the chief, his small band and their summer expeditions. What an innocent time. Roy left this earth in the summer of 2014. I have so many more questions to ask him and am so grateful that he shared his stories with me. Roy is survived by his wife of 60 years, Toot. As I said earlier, both are wonderful historians about South Whidbey and Columbia Beach. I came to spend many hours asking them about the cottage, the beach, about the two owners - Berte, Wil and Lucille.

The Restoration

Time went by quickly from the auction to the real estate closing, the event that formalized my ownership of the cottage. I did a lot of thinking about the cottage and my intentions for it became clearer as I approached the 60 day deadline to come up with the cash to make the purchase. When June 7 came and went, with it came a change in how I felt about the cottage. Initially I walked through the cottage with a touch but do not disturb mentality. I did not look in depth. I had only been in the cottage two times following the auction, once with my son and once with my family members. Now I felt as if I had the right to really look and explore the contents. This is when I found Wil's journals.

The journals had been laying right in the open and looked most likely to be a couple of note pads for such activities as making lists for the grocery store or for a project. None of the journals looked like the diaries that they were. I almost threw them out. There were many old newspapers and magazines in several places in the cottage. The wood box contained a stack of newspapers from the 1950's and 60's. The McCarthy trials of the 1950's, the World's Fair in Seattle - a 1963 event were headlines. There were multiple magazines from the 1950's. Interesting that there were no new newspapers or magazines or any printed matter from the previous 25 years except tide books. After reading several editions, I eventually gave the antique literature to a collector.

My first big task was to clear away the clutter, junk and unusable items found throughout the house and in the garage. This was a massive undertaking and I contacted a "picker" to haul away a dump truck worth of trash. In that trash was the collapsed garage. As mentioned earlier, it was halfway submerged into the dirt, an outcome of a landslide that had occurred 20+ years earlier and the county elevating the road by over a foot. The garage was leaning substantially to one side and was missing major parts of its roof. The wood had not been painted in so long that it appeared weathered and grey. It did not take much to get it to collapse. The picker walked through the house with Bryan and me; I indicated all that I wished to keep. He pretty much stuck to that, although a few things did disappear. I wasn't about to get worried about that. He had two men with him along with his wife and working all at one time like a swarm of bees, they emptied the cottage and swept away the pile of old wood debris from the garage. When the truck drove off, I breathed a sigh of relief. It literally felt as if a heavy weight had been lifted off my chest and I felt lighter.

There still were several items left in the cottage that I needed to deal with before I could begin repairing the cottage. I kept the two bedroom storage pieces - the tall bureau and the dressing table. There were 5 small end tables that were found amongst the living room and bedroom spaces. I kept the kitchen table but not the chairs. Whether I ended up keeping the kitchen table or not, it would prove to be very useful during the repair phase. Those 8 pieces were all that I kept in terms of furniture. I also kept the linens, the kitchen canisters and the salt & pepper shaker collection. A few miscellaneous curio pieces were kept along with a bunch of fishing gear and I kept the case of "Diamond" round

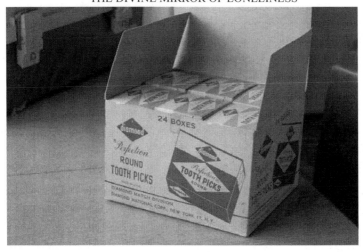

toothpicks! I wrapped them up and sent them to my cousin for Christmas the following holiday season. She still has them - they pretty much are a "lifetime supply".

This all happened the week after I took possession of the cottage - the middle of June. When Bryan and I drove away from the cottage that day, I was consumed with "next steps". How was I going to repair this cottage? There most definitely was a lot of work to be done and not all of it could be done by myself. I needed help. Help came in the form of 4 people - my cousin Fran wasted no time in volunteering to help and she was a huge help. My son Bryan helped, especially with the heavy lifting - moving dirt, gravel, paving stones, furniture, etc. He used the big machinery for me such as the floor sander. As I mentioned before, every floor in the cottage was wood. Not all of it was in good condition and all of it needed to be sanded. He also helped with the pressure washer. Between the two of us we pressure washed the entire exterior of the cottage, to remove the flaked and peeling paint and ready it for a new coat of primer and paint. The other two individuals were Mike my retired architect neighbor and his twin brother Dan, retired from a career as a structural engineer building bridges all around the world. What fantastic workers and craftsmen they are and what a difference they made for the outcome of the cottage renewal. Each of those four people contributed significantly to the outcome of the cottage and to what it is today and for that I will be forever grateful.

Mike and Dan treated it as a job. They would report down there and begin work after morning coffee and work a significant number of hours. They worked on demolition and carpentry tasks such as replacing bug-destroyed flooring, outside trim, painting both inside and out and whatever they did, it was done with precision and quality. I was still employed, so I was not able to be down there most of the time they were working. It was wonderful that I didn't have to worry with them on the job.

Second bedroom after renovation

For the rest of the work, I hired contractors. Amazingly, they were there daily until the work was done. I have come to understand that this is not always the way on the "island" as "island time" is often observed. The year - 2012 might have had something to do with it. Work on the island was not abundant at that time as the "Great Recession" had taken its toll. We began work the first week of July 2012 and finished by November of that year. The transformation was amazing. I can say it was thoroughly enjoyable, although hard work. It was a big, complex project - the type I love to be involved in.

Every surface of the cottage, inside and out was touched. All walls, floors and ceilings were primed and painted. One bedroom had two layers of wallpaper plus a foundation of cardboard over cedar wall boards. It was stripped down to the cedar and painted cream white as the rest of the cottage would be soon. My cousin Fran and I tackled that job - it took us the majority of two days.

The underneath of the cottage was totally revived, repaired and lastly, insulated. The roof was replaced and insulated. The stove and refrigerator were replaced. All of the kitchen cabinets, countertop, sinks both kitchen/bath as well as the bathtub were saved and restored.

The restored living room

All of the windows were removed, re-glazed, primed and painted in the turquoise green color and replaced. All of the doors were saved and new exterior locks were added. The porches were repaired. New lighting fixtures and smoke detectors were added and all the knob and tube wiring was replaced.

The exterior was primed and then painted a "Creamsicle Orange" color - that plus the turquoise green trim on the windows and white fascia and trim on the house made it a truly "beachy" cottage. It was very playful and happy - as it should be. The yard needed gravel paths and cement stepping stones to allow walking around in the winter and avoiding the wet ground that often had to handle all the water from the neighbor's runoff. It worked perfectly.

The foundation contractor suggested we scrape the top off of the large mound of dirt in the yard next to the beach and add cement blocks to the top for a patio. A perfect solution to those 36 yards of dirt dropped there in 1977. Wil had the intention to move it around the yard but it was such a big job, he was overwhelmed and the grass eventually grew over it. Some thought it was a septic "mound" from that style of septic systems installed in the 80's and 90's but my neighbors Toot and Roy told me differently and so did Wil in his journal.

The grass in the yard undulates with the sinking and settling of sand and logs and is quite green most of the year. In the front or street side, we took down the old garage that could no longer be parked in as it had sustained damage and a lot of mud from an earlier mudslide and then the raising of the road by the county. We didn't have to do much to take it down as it basically fell down when approached. We had already removed all objects worth saving and all that was left was a pile of old lumber. Now we had a place to put a path down to the cottage and a small white picket fence. The "look" and my vision were now one and the same.

The Creamsicle Cottage - from vision to reality

It became apparent in the wet winter that we needed to install some sort of parking area in the front yard because it turned quite muddy and folks who attempted to park there would get stuck in the mud. This situation was quite dangerous and definitely a mess! A "landscape wall" was added, filled with gravel and it is now a very safe parking area for up to 4 cars.

The beach at the edge of the backyard - was then and is now still full of huge driftwood logs. Those logs arrived in 2003 during a particularly wet and windy storm and resulting mudslide that moved over a thousand logs into the water at the south end of the island. They remain there today, decaying giants representing outcast timber from a once vibrant and healthy forest along the shore. My challenge was "how do I get to the beach through all these logs?" It was not an easy solution. Initially my neighbor to the north said we could walk through their beach alongside of their cement bulkhead, but when they decided to put their house up for sale, they no longer wanted us to use it. So we tackled carving a path with brute strength and a chainsaw the following year and have done so each spring as the logs tend to move around during winter high tides and storms.

Columbia Beach and the ferry

11 THE MAGIC WITHIN

Berte Olson, the first female ferry boat captain was probably the first occupant of the cottage. The next occupant was her sister. I know that Berte was a very strong woman who was known to "tip a few" and had a mind of her own. I don't know much about her sister. The cottage was sold to Wil and Lucille in 1954. It seemed that they had good times, at least in the first 10 or 15 years. Wil ended his time in the cottage suddenly and for many of the years was shrouded in loneliness. His sad and lonely presence after he left this earth was noted by a spiritual medium who visited the cottage one day. Other than that sad presence, there is a very happy energy in the cottage. It is happy to just look at. In addition, all the wonderful experiences that have taken place there in the past 4 years by very happy souls, young and old alike, fill the cottage with positive energy.

Jill Johnston, the island story teller and performer has written and performed a story titled "Little, But Oh My" about Berte Olson. She was invited to tell her story in the cottage and obliged to the delight of a room full of people. Her tale and mini-performance right there in the cottage was magical. Folks have come from California, Oregon and Minnesota to enjoy the cottage. The 4th of July celebration enjoyed by family and friends just had its 4th annual happening. I have extended an open invitation to the cottage to any of my friends and family who wish to enjoy it. It is busy every weekend during the summer. Each visitor has contributed something to the cottage - items for the kitchen, some bought and some hand-painted or hand-sewn. Art for the walls, videos and CD's for rainy days, barbeque and tools for outdoor grilling. Tools for the yard, crab pots and crab crackers for the annual two months of crabbing. Marshmallow sticks for the fire pit and S'Mores. Food and drink to share. Most of all, they brought their love and enjoyment and shared all that with me. What joyful times. I believe that Wil and Lucille smile upon us and upon the once again, happy cottage from their place in the heavens.

Many lovely evenings we find ourselves sitting at the picnic table on the patio during a warm evening as the sun sets below the hillside in the west. The moon rises over the Cascade mountains to the east and casts its moonbeam across the still water to where we sit. There is no other feeling like that in the world.

In the middle of a hot August afternoon, I walk out with a cool beverage in hand and my dog Chester in tow. We set the beach umbrella up over the Adirondack chair on the patio and have a seat, me on the chair and Chester on my lap. Together we contemplate the world.

The ferry crosses our vision behind the gently waving American flag and a cool breeze slips under my visor and across my toes as I stretch out. The heat of the day no longer "too hot" and the chill off the water no longer "too cold". Everything is perfect. How lovely is that and how lucky am I?

I often thank Wil and Lucille at times like this. I know how much he especially loved the cottage. I also know that he died within a month of my purchase of the cottage. I think he was hanging onto life to get back to his beloved cottage. I have worked very hard to honor all that he loved about the cottage and to honor his work and life there. His journey has similarities to mine in a very poignant way. The loneliness is something I have dealt with and continue to deal with. What was revealed to me in his journals gives me a very different perspective on life and has allowed me to view my thoughts and decisions in a very different way, causing a change in outcomes for me. I will always be thankful to that silent man for this change in my life.

12   LIFE CAPTURED

I was most fortunate to have acquired the cottage. For its location on a beautiful beach and for all the history and treasures found within. The discovery of the journals gave context and meaning to the cottage and so much of what I found inside. The journals told the story of the cottage, of history and of life from one man's point-of-view. Rarely are we afforded such context and I knew what I had found in the five journals was indeed special. I read the journals thoroughly from cover-to-cover three times. Two of those times very carefully. It was a wonderful journey through time. I did notice several themes to Wil's writing that you might watch for.

Theme 1: Wil is an avid fisherman and so was Lucille. Much of the writing in his journals has to do with fishing. What was caught, how many, on which lure, at what time of day and where. Mostly that information catalogued what he and Lucille caught, but often he catalogues what others were catching as well. I have edited much of that dialogue out of what I will share here because even though those entries and that information might be of great interest to a local fisherperson, to this story it is only one aspect. You will still get the feeling for his love of fishing in what I have elected to include.

Theme 2: Wil includes significant events of weather, politics, the economy and happenings that would have appeared in the news. Most of that information I have included in the story. I chose to include it because Wil has a reaction to it. Those events shaped his experience and feelings and around those events he frequently shared his values and feelings. It also anchors your perspective of time when you see "Record Attendance At World's Fair" or "Mt. St. Helen's Erupted Today" in his writing. I enjoy reflecting in my own history and allowing both myself and the reader to reflect and think about where was I at that time in history?

Theme 3: Wil lived life in detail and recorded specifics he wanted to remember, such as the brand name, model number, paint color and cost of items he used. He was very careful to include all information. I have left a sampling of the details throughout the selections I am sharing with you. There is much more in the original journals and while it would have painted a picture of a very meticulous person, that level of detail would have been redundant and probably less interesting to the reader. In most cases, I do include the whole journal entry for a particular day as I believe the array of topics is in itself informative. I did not pick a single sentence to share with you from a much larger entry. His entries were not overly long. Toward the last ten years of his life, they became shorter and shorter.

Theme 4: Wil also passes 57 years of his life owning the cottage and 51 years were captured in five journals. You will see the impact of an advancing world on this man in his mid-thirties through to his mid-eighties. The 1960's through the early 2000's was an age of advancing technology, increasing population and rising inflation. From the changes in his job as a telephone lineman, the communication devices he owned, the cars/trucks he drove and the once quiet neighborhoods he lived in - they all experienced rapid advancement and change. He felt his world was slipping away and he was often angry about it. You will see this in his writing. You will also see his view of the changes taking place in his body. The things he can no longer do. The accommodations he has to make with his physical body. Sometimes humorous, often poignant.

Theme 5: Much of the journal writing is documenting Wil's caring for the cottage. It is almost as if by recording what he did to maintain, improve and repair the cottage, he established reason for being there. Or perhaps those events were easier to document and write about. Continuous references to plumbing leaks, repair of missing shingles on the roof, shoring up (chinking) the bulkhead, removing logs that were clogging his beach, mowing the lawn, painting both the interior and exterior of the cottage as well as dealing with mudslides, a sagging foundation, malfunctioning oil heater and broken kitchen appliances. Winterizing meant draining the water heater, pipes and toilet and adding anti-freeze to prevent freezing in the winter. That was followed several months later by reversing the procedure in the late spring. There were many references to not turning the water on because it was not past the danger of freezing. On those occasions he would use the portable toilet at the nearby park and the outside water spigot.

Theme 6: The last grouping of information is made up of the people in Wil's life. His family, friends and neighbors and most specifically his wife Lucille. Observe the evolution of relationships as the years and experiences over time shape his thoughts, his fears and his frustrations. Wil chronicles illness and death of those around him. Note the activities Wil and Lucille engaged in together in those early years - the fishing, boating, travel to and from the cottage, clamming, painting and golfing. Then observe the gradual disappearance of activity and growing physical distance between the two of them as the years progress. The increase in number of vacations Lucille takes with her daughter, relatives and friends and his reactions to those times of her absence from his life. In particular, note how one-by-one his circle of friends and family becomes smaller and smaller.

These journals started five years after Wil and Lucille bought the cottage. What caused him to begin the process of journaling is unknown. Wil actually called them "logs", like a "captains log". He appears to have been quite faithful in making written entries on most of his visits, possibly on all visits. Because I have only included a selected sample of journal entries, it will not be as evident to you that as he became older, the visits to the cottage were further and further apart, especially in the winter when it was very hard to be in the cottage because of the cold temperatures and lack of water. His activities at the cottage amazingly were very similar over the years. He still ventured on top of the roof to tack down a tarp or weave in a few shingles and went under the cottage to shore up a sagging foundation. He talks about it in his journals and the neighbors I spoke with said it was amazing to see this elderly man doing these tasks. What he did give up was fishing and golf, perhaps because Lucille was not there and also most likely because it was difficult to launch a boat alone and he no longer had friends (or Lucille) to golf with.

All the passages I have elected to use here are word-for-word what Wil wrote. I have selected a sub-set of entries representative of the 51 year total to make it more concise for you the reader. What you cannot see, because I transcribed his journals onto the computer, is the volume of writing and the neatness of his block printing. Also you cannot see how both the volume and length of entries, as well as the printing itself change over time. In the end it is very wobbly and the entries are very brief. Wil did not know that his entry on 10-15-2010 would be his last. His first occurred nearly 51 years before that date on 6-17-1959. You and I are privileged to have a unique view of 51 years of life through the personal lens of a very quiet man.

Interwoven throughout Wil's transcribed entries I have interjected the voice of Berte Olsen. Berte's presence is still very strong in the little wooden cottage. I felt it the first time I was alone in it. You can almost smell the burning Alder wood in the wood stove, heating the cottage and then the aroma of the thick stew simmering in a cast iron pot on top of the stove. The ceilings and doorways are low and that didn't matter to Berte, she wasn't even 5' tall. The windows throughout were simple wooden sliders that sat in a 2" groove, with one window capable of being slid from one side-to-the other. In order to work on the windows, repaint and reglaze each pane, I took out the stationary windows as well as the sliders. This could be done by removing the exterior trim of the window which gave me access to the whole window. When one of the stationary windows in the kitchen was removed, I noticed a dark disk about the size of a quarter on the sill. I suspected it might be a quarter although it was totally black. I picked it up and when I got around to cleaning it I found it to be a 1925 Standing Lady quarter. It was as if Berte wanted me to know someone had been there so long ago. And a "Standing Lady", how appropriate!

As you read Wil's journal entries, Berte interjects herself to provide information, humor and thoughts common to the era in which she and Wilbur lived and beyond.

Enjoy this journey through time.

13 UNOFFICIAL JOURNAL #0

A small, spiral-bound notebook was amongst a box of hardware and "junk drawer" items that were moved to my house before renovation of the cottage began in June of 2012. It wasn't until July of 2016 that I actually discovered this small, sparse journal. It covers 3 years of Wil and Lucille's ownership of the cottage, from June 1959 to June 1962. It begins five years after Wil and Lucille bought the cottage in 1954. This appears to be Wil's first attempt at keeping notes about his experiences in life, there are few entries and most are far apart in time. Here is also where I am going to interject the voice of Berte Olson, the original owner of the small fishing cottage. *Her voice will be in "italics".*

First entry:

6-17-1959 <u>Berte died.</u>

I didn't realize it mattered to him, my death. My sister Helena sold him and his wife that little wooden cottage 5 years ago. Oh, I had memories in that cottage, some good and some not-so-good. It was built well you know. The local boys used fir and cedar from the mill over along the Skykomish slough for both the inside and out. The original cabin only had one bedroom and no bathroom, just an outhouse out back that was pretty darn cold in the winter. Those winters of the late 1920's and early 30's were cold and damp. There was only the wood-burning stove to keep you warm, cook food and boil the water for a bath. Life was pretty tough for my sisters and me growing up. My husband and me worked real hard building that ferry route from Anacortes to Whidbey and then the state and the feds built a bridge right over that treacherous water known as Deception Pass and our ferry was no longer needed. My husband also decided that I was no longer needed and left me that winter. There was no time to sulk, I had to earn a living, times were tough in the mid-30's with the Great Depression and all. I was a fireball, doing what I set out to do and pretty damned independent as well. They called me "strong-willed and colorful". I can say that I drank a bit in those days. Hell, I drank quite a bit if I am being truthful. Probably what they meant when they called me "colorful"! Well that and my language now and then. Don't see no point in not being truthful at this point - I'm dead and gone! Now ain't that some sort of statement!

The set-back of losing the Whidbey ferry route and my husband all at the same time didn't keep me from moving on. I convinced Alexander Peabody, the president of the Black Ball Line (became the Washington State Ferries) to sell me the franchise for the Port Gamble-Shine ferry run on Hood Canal. From that, I created my own ferry boat business, the Olympic Navigation Company. That route did me very well for many years then they started talking about putting in a floating bridge right across that stretch of water. Imagine that - a bridge that floats! Well I'll be damned. That talk started in 1951 and that bridge was up in 1961. They started construction in 1958, just before I died.

When I moved to the Hood Canal route I packed up my cabin, belongings and all and barged it over for me and my kids to live close to the new run. I did the same thing to the little cabin I brought down for my sister. I 'barged' it down to Columbia Beach on the east side of Whidbey. We added two big logs to the bottom of the cabin that became "skids" for dragging it across the beach right up to where it now sits. My sister Inga had a home there and we set it right next to her piece of land. My other sister Helena moved into it and we added a bedroom and a bathroom to make it nice for her. I spent my childhood years in Clinton, right near where I took that little cabin. I thought about coming back to those parts of Whidbey and living near my sisters, but it never happened.

Helena sold the cabin in July of 1954 and died a year later in August of 1955. At that time, the deed to the cottage came back to me and 5 years later, after I died in 1959, it was signed over to Wilbur and Lucille Mills when they paid off the contract in May of 1960. So it was never to be that I would again live in the small island community of Clinton that I knew so well.

I'm still there you know. You can't see me, but I sit in the kitchen of that little wooden cottage, looking out the window at the boats and the fishermen. I loved the sea. The smell of the beach and the water that filled the air, the fresh cold mist that would blanket my face during a morning ferry run. The sound of the ships' bell in the fog and the salt water slapping against the sides of my boat. It all takes me back to those times that are etched into my soul. The sea is a part of me now. I will never leave it. It makes me feel good to see Wil and Lucille enjoying this cottage so much. He takes great care of it, much better than I used to take care of my cabin. And that young girl Tootie comes over to babysit Lucille's child now and then. I like her - she even scrubs the floors when she babysits. Now that is my sort of work ethic. I heard that Tootie married some great big, tall guy and she came back to live on Columbia Beach with him, his name was LeeRoy Young. Nice folk.

6-18-1959 Came up by myself. Lucille's dad is sick. Still painting boats. 22# King caught at Jim-Johns today.

6-19-1959 Lucille has had hay fever quite severely for 2 weeks. Picked up 1959 Ford.

6-29-1959 Came to Whidbey in new auto. 114 miles on it already. Windy, wet weather. Just finished part of mountain job. Now pulling cable on hwy 99.

6-30-1959 Came up by myself. Lucille's dad, mom and brother-in-law are sick. Painted dinghy bottom. Poor weather so far this year.

7-4-1959 Painted 2nd coat on dinghy and copper paint on Birchcraft. Barbequed corn and steak.

7-5-1959 Rougher than the proverbial cob. Small craft warnings are up.

7-11-1959 Tied boat out after 2nd copper coat. Painted front room "Sun Tan". Used ½ gallon. $6.80 per gal, $1.75 tray.

8-31-1959 Caught 1 Humpie. Fish was marked. Rained Tues. Lucille caught 1 Silver - a 7 pounder at Glendale. Netted 1 Humpie also in front of house.

Wil and Lucille really enjoy fishing. If you don't know much about fishing, a humpie is a "throwback" or "fertilizer" fish. You don't keep them unless you don't know better. They are kinda mushy and don't taste as good as others. King and Silvers are the best.

9-6-1959 Caught a beauty at 7:00 AM, about 12# on frozen Herring. No fresh bait.

10-17-1959 Lucille quit job at packing company.

10-18-1959 Pulled boat up with car. Real nice weather, some fog.

10-24-1959 Had molar pulled by dentist. $5.00.

10-25-1959 Nice sunny day, light frost in morning. Pulled anchor line, buck and chain. Cliff pulled anchor into spar during week, recovered anchor on a low tide. Beautiful moonlit, chilly night.

10-27-1959 Next year we need a new anchor block.

1-1-1960 Car stolen, Dec. 29, 1959.

1-3-1960 Came up, 23 degrees last night, 30 degrees at noon today

6-2-1960 Lucille has hay fever or asthma quite bad.

6-26-1960 Used skin suit for first time. Lots of fun.

4-15-1962 Turned on water (inside the cottage), sanded boat. Ed Leaf bought 20' Tollycraft.

4-16-1962 World's Fair opens next week. Maridel is now a sophomore at Cheney. Was at Eastern Washington State University.

I've noticed Will writing in his little notebook - not many entries for a whole year but you will come to see that he starts writing more entries as time goes by. Soon he writes every time he is up at the cottage. It is interesting to me to notice what he chooses to write down. He is quite detailed about some things and other things he only writes a couple words. His entry about my death - 'Berte died'. That was all he said. Well I might have hoped that I was worthy of more than two words but then I guess I was surprised that he even knew about my dying. You will see that he

73

keeps detailed notes about fishing - the time, tide, temperature, lure, bait, species, length and weight of what was caught (or not). I suppose he is one of those sorts of people who live in details. I find that manner of living life can be pretty difficult and very tiring. I didn't live in details, I always stood back and looked at the big picture. If I let the small stuff bother me, I would have had a heck of a time running a ferry boat.

14 JOURNAL NUMBER 1

This log is an actual spiral-bound notebook-sized journal, 8.5 x 11 format but less than ¼ inch thick. It covers nearly ten years, from June 1962 until March of 1972. Wil and Lucille will experience their late 30's and early 40's during this time.

6-10-1962 Launched Birchcraft & fished with F.S.T., no luck. Hull requires about 1 qt. of bottom paint for 2 coats. Used a white paint with less gloss this year. Lucille still has hay fever, although not as bad as in May. Coldest May on record this year. Used 25' of ½" line & 35' of ¾" line purchased at Shinners $7.00 for ¾" & $2.50 for ½".

8-12-1962 Trolled for 4 hrs. over weekend without much success. The electrician caught two 20 pounders on the west side of Hat Island. They were caught on the low slack at 9:00 a.m. on plugs. Maridel sold her '54 Chev for $175. She purchased a '58 Plymouth Fury.

Maridel or M.D. for short is Wil's step-daughter, Lucille's daughter. Wil seems to observe her from afar, doesn't get very involved in her life. Perhaps she wants it that way, after all, he isn't her father. Or perhaps he wants it that way or doesn't have a clue how to relate to her. It seems that Wil is not the best relationship-builder.

9-30-1962 Lucille mooched out front in the dinghy, caught 2 lb. Blackmouth.

10-2-1962 Birchcraft went adrift. Ed & Inga recovered it, and pulled it up in yard. Tug & logs ran over the line.

10-6-1962 Attended World Fair on record attendance day (106,000).

10-7-1962 We came up with Lucille's mother to see about boat. Rainy stormy weather.

10-12-1962 Worst wind storm in N.W. history. Winds ranged from 90 to 140 M.P.H. I was sent to Albany, Ore. for a week to help restore service. Our planks were washed away.

11-4-1962 Closed Whidbey. It rained today for the first time since the Oct. 12 storm. The wind was over 10 knots for the first time also. We have new neighbors to the north of us.

3-9 - 1963 Beautiful weather this past week. Morning fog & sunshine. Wil mowed lawn. Lucille & M.D. went to Cottage Grove (Oregon).

6-8/9 - 1963 Bought some used 4" x 12" x 12' planks. They were recovered by General Const. Co. dismantling Pier 46 in Seattle. They cost $80.00 per thousand board feet. We purchased 6 planks for $23.00. We then constructed our first ramp, after ten years, what a challenge! Painted bottom of Birchcraft. Saw man flip boat & motor.

June 29/30 - 1963 Lucille's mother came up from Oregon. Painted back door 2nd coat, Chinese Green #281. They raced around Whidbey today. Good percentage of finishers were fiberglass.

July 13-14 - 1963 I caught one 3# Blackmouth on plug with cut herring near Glendale at 3 p.m. Lorna is now married. She had dinner with us as Inga was not home. Maridel is just another unemployed statistic. Summer has been quite damp so far. My teeth are now 10 days old as I acquired them July 2nd, 1963.

8-4-1963 Came up by myself to mow lawn. Mr. Young has copied me by purchasing store bought teeth. The fishing this past week is nothing short of spectacular. A commercial fishing strike may have something to do with it.

9-10-1963 I wired a new circuit into the master bedroom this week at a cost of $2.50. Lucille's rug is now laid at a cost of $539.00! It is a "Downs Gingham Fair".

10-6-1963 Pulled boat up with triple sheaves. Someone had been using it. Lucille has asthma again today.

11-10-1963 Patched shingles around foundation post. Filled in some dirt around bulkhead. We have gained 1 ½ feet of new sand on the beach. Lucille is dubious about her job. GMC needs front tires.

12-30-1963 Everything A.OK. New Hawaiian neighbors on the north. I have had a rather serious cold the past week and a half. Blackmouth are biting out front.

2-2-1964 January was one of the wettest on record. Consequently we suffered from the inevitable slide and high tide. Groundhog saw his shadow today.

Thought I would tell you about the geography of this island. Except for the north end of the island around Deception Pass where I had my ferry boat run, and Fidalgo Island where my cabin and the cottage were built and I lived, the island is made up mostly of sand and glacial til (rocks, dirt, etc. moved and deposited by a glacier)and it regularly slides from the edges or bluffs down onto the beaches where it eventually ends up in the water. This is a natural thing but if you were dumb enough to build a cabin on the beach too close to a steep bluff or build a cabin too close to the edge at the top of a bluff - when it slides, you lose your cabin. This still goes on and it always will. Too much rain with freezing and thawing makes things in those bluffs happen, so winter and early spring are when you get the slides. The area of Whidbey I put the cabin on, Columbia Beach, is one of the areas that is always getting slides from the bluffs above and sand moving onto the beach from other beaches and landslides. The sand can also disappear from a beach during storms or heavy currents. You get used to it but it isn't something you like because it causes a lot of damage and things change. You can't get from the beach to your beach ramp or your cabin is hit by a slide and you end up with a huge pile of mud and trees covering your yard. Wil had this happen more than once and he sure didn't like it. One of his neighbors two houses south, had the mudslide come off the hill behind his house, burst into his garage, right under his car and lifted that car 4 feet into the air! It was one of those fancy sport cars - a Corvette. Boy that was something!

4-5-1964 Came up to see if the Alaska Good Friday tidal wave affected our property. The wave was insignificant in the Sound, so we are A. OK.

8-2-1964 Lucille painted the trim on the cabin. The weather has been beautiful for the past two weeks. The island is developing so fast, there are more real estate salesman than deer on the island.

Well they've owned the cottage for 10 years now. Glad to see they are keeping it in shape. It seems Lucille has quite a time with allergies and asthma. I think Whidbey Island has been 'discovered' so-to-speak. Of course there is a ferry that brings folks right here to Columbia Beach - it is known as the 'Mukilteo-Columbia Beach run'. These ferries are much bigger than mine was. Mine only held 12 - 16 cars and cost 50 cents for car and driver. But mine was the first ferry run to Whidbey Island, that was in 1919. The Acorn and the Deception were part of the 'Mosquito Fleet' - a collection of smaller ferries that served ports all over Puget Sound.

11-15-1964 Drained pipes, closed up shop. Am splicing at Issaquah 6 days per week, 9 ½ hrs. per day.

6-6-1965 Maridel was married 2 weeks ago, Saturday. We have purchased a '58 Skagit 16' '59 Mercury 35A and '60 Montgomery Ward trailer. We launched at the Mukilteo boat house for the first time. Lucille was bitten by a spider today.

8-15-1965 We have trailed our boat to Mukilteo 5 times. No fish as yet. Am splicing at Kent for a couple weeks. Namu was captured this summer. He's a killer whale.

8-31-1965 Lucille caught an 8lb. Humpie at 8:00 this morning. High tide change. The commercial fisherman are not allowed to fish here yet. A lot of fish have been caught this past week.

9-2-1965 Lucille has been out-fishing me in our new boat. I bought her a brand spanking new white dodger. Lucille then proceeded to catch the 12 pounder and limited the next day with the two 10 lb'ers and a 6 lb. Blackmouth. She did all this while steering the boat. I'm looking for a new hobby.

Well dang! Wil has a sense of humor! It doesn't show itself very much, but it is underneath that quiet, nit-pickin exterior. You might wonder what a 'dodger' is - well it is a flat piece of flashy metal painted various colors to attract the attention of the fish. It is attached to the line along with weights and the hook set-up.

7-3-1966 The summer is cool and wet. This three day weekend has had lots of rain. Lucille has hay fever. Ole bought a place at Lagoon Point. Boeings is planning to locate north of Paine Field. The speculators are here in great numbers.

Ahhhh, the reason for the increased interest in Whidbey Island - Boeing is expanding and building an assembly plant in Everett! You know, Seattle is known as a 'one-horse town' - Boeing is the biggest game around here and when Boeing is up, things are booming, when it is down times are tough. Once right after a big Boeing lay-off in 1971, they posted a billboard right on the freeway near the airport and it said, 'Will the last person leaving Seattle - turn out the lights?', now that was quite a statement! Unemployment in the area was 13% after that layoff. Of course that won't happen for 5 years as it is only 1966 in Wil's journal right now. Ain't it grand to be able to see into the future? One of the perks of being dead.

7-23-1966   First full weekend we've had in quite a while. Doing a lot of work at the Boeing Space Center and Auburn.

Aug/Sept-1966 Caught 7 fish on vacation. Lucille caught 4, I caught remainder.

9-30-1967 The weather this summer was the best in years. Day after day of above 80 degree weather. We purchased Gregg's sailing dinghy and 2 H.P. Elgin. M.D. and Scott have sold our '59 Ford. They now each have a '65 Corvette.

11-5-1967 We turned off the water today. The weather has been superb this weekend. Inga's place is for sale. She is asking $18,500! I have a new calendar wrist watch. Self-winding, 17 jewels.

Oh I'm a bit sad, Inga was family. She lived in the house just south of Wil and Lucille. A lot of changes coming.

12-28-1967 Came up to check after effects of a 14'6" high tide (highest in 62 years). We weathered the situation in fine form. Had a lovely Christmas at Bud & Bonnies. 1500 more employees will come to Paine Field (Everett) after the first of the year.

3-24-1968 Mowed lawn. Lucille came up for the first time this year. Taffy was killed by a dump truck this spring. We both have colds. Inga's place has been sold.

4-22-1968 I am now on strike. Our AFL-CIO strike started April 18th. Mowed lawn & sprayed caterpillars. Ed is ill. Lucille now wears glasses and has a wig.

Interesting commentary, Lucille and Wil are in their mid-forties now. Wil always notes both changes and conditions of Lucille, then he goes on noting facts such as 'sprayed for caterpillars' as each are facts and events of that day and they seem equally important in the log. I don't suppose he really felt that way but that side of him that is so doggoned factual just can't help himself.

5-19-1968 Mowed lawn. Strike is now over. It lasted 18 days. We both wear glasses now. Lucille got a 5 speed Schwinn bike for her birthday. My temporary anchor block drifted away.

8-25-1968 Changed the bedrails in the master bedroom using rails from Kent house. We are having the wettest August in history. The salmon fishing has been great for the charters. We haven't even wet a line this year.

9-1-1968 Re-shingled the west bedroom on the north half of roof. It required a little over 4 bundles. Shingles are getting scarce due to the Japs buying all the good Cedar. Scott and M.D. came up on the 7th and 8th. Scott and I scuba dove.

11-3-1968 Turned water off. Mowed lawn. We have more new neighbors to the north. Mrs. Leaf is quite ill in a hospital in Everett. Need to replace 3 more posts under house. Scott is on a ten day hunting trip !!

Wil talks about replacing posts under the cottage. This will become something that Will engages in for the next 40 years - until he is nearly 85 years old. When I barged this cabin down to this piece of land, it was placed upon a set of posts and beams, a typical type of foundation for those times. The space under the cottage is about 24" at most. For such a tall man, working in this confined, wet and cold space had to be difficult. Me? I'm only 4'11' tall and getting in and out of small spaces was easy.

1-4-1969 Came up for the first time this year. Lucille now has an automatic garage door opener. So far we've had a lot of snow and freezing weather this winter.

2-9-1969 January was one of the worst in 20 years for snowfall and freezing. Came up to chink bulkhead. The 747 took off today.

3-2-1969 Still chinking the bulkhead. The Cascades are spectacular today due to all the January snow. Scott & M.D. just got back from a ski vacation lasting a week at Big Mountain, Montana. Pruned the rose today.

One thing you learn quick when you work or live near or on the sea is that you have to give respect to her power. She can carry you where you need to go just as easy as she can destroy you and your possessions. Wil had to constantly mend the bulkhead, the main protection between the sea and the cottage. He also had to work to keep his access to the beach which meant removing large logs brought in by the water from his ramp and bulkhead. The process of chinking meant filling the spaces between the bulkhead pilings that were pounded into the sand. When those pilings stood side-by-side they formed a wall between the sea and his yard, much the same as you would chink a log cabin - fill the spaces between the logs with some hard material.

5-18-1969 We have just had 2 weeks of perfect weather. We finally traded the old GMC in! It had 98,000 on it and still was using 20 weight oil! We traded it for a '66 Chevy ½ ton. It has 32,300 on it. We visited Ethel last weekend at Cottage Grove.

Ethel is a relative. I don't think I've heard Wil talk of any other relatives other than Lucille's daughter Maridel.

5-30-1969 Ethel is extremely ill. We visited her in the Cottage Grove hospital over the Memorial Day Weekend.

6-1-8-1969 Spent my first weeks' vacation at Whidbey. Benny is still in Vietnam. They have built a new ferry slip. The ferry boats now land further north.

8-24-1969 It was rough on Sunday. Four ferries are now on the Mukilteo-Columbia Beach run. They are the good ships Chetzemoka, Olympic, Rhododendron and Skansonia.

9-11-1969 Our vacation is rapidly drawing to a close. We had superb weather. Restrictions on catching Humpies were imposed this year due to the 1967 floods damaging the spawning grounds. We only caught two fish. We golfed at Useless Bay this year.

12-20-1969 This winter has been much milder than last. Ed has been very ill with circulatory problems. We have a new topless ferry.

1-11-1970 Worked on bulkhead. Lucille hauled sand while I chinked.

2-22-1970 Had to re-chink bulkhead. Weather still beautiful. Lucille cracked ankle bone skiing. I tried to tell her.

3-8-1970 Lucille still limping. This has been a beautiful winter weather wise. Still re-chinking bulkhead.

4-19-1970 Came down from Port Townsend. Cemented bulkhead. Ed had mowed lawn. M.D. is P.G.

Well, if you are not familiar with that term, 'P.G.' meant pregnant. This is the only child Maridel gives birth to and the only grandchild for Lucille and Wil.

4-25-1970 Skin dove for the first time this year. Am still working at Port Townsend. We also golfed a 9 hole round at Useless Bay. M.D. is still P.G.

5-23-1970 Golfed all weekend. Lost a dozen balls - too many slices.

6-8-1970 Lucille pulled a low blow on me by going back to work a week before my spring vacation, hence I spend a wifeless vacation!

6-21-1970 85 degree weather. We are quite sun burned. I received a beautiful golf cart & anchor buoy for Fathers' Day.

6-27-1970 Still can't start Mercury. Poured cement base for porch. Chinked bulkhead. M.D. is still P.G.

7-11-1970 M.D. and Scott came up to golf. Good weather.

7-18-1970 Weather still good, tremendous summer for boating. Forest fire danger is omnipresent on the scene.

8-16-1970 Mercury still running beautifully after its tune-up. We golfed again! Lucille tied me with a 66 for 9. Young is putting the finishing touches on his bulkhead. I am working in Olympia.

10-10-1970 Came up by myself. Watched World Series game. Baltimore beat Cincinnati 6-5. Looks like they are building a couple of taverns on the Mukilteo Speedway. That's all we need.

10-24-1970 Mowed lawn. Came to get Skagit. Am going back to Auburn garage. Economic situation is miserable in the northwest.

There see! Remember what I told you about Boeing laying off folks and the bill board that went up in 1971? Well we are almost there and things don't look good.

11-27-1970 M.D. finally had her baby. C. J. Jr. (Chris) 8-2 lb. Cold clear day. Our water pipe seems to be leaking near the meter.

7-7-1971 Weather this year has been miserable, only a handful of warm days. We are still golf bugs. Our low scores are 53 & 60 at Holmes Harbor. Lucille broke the oar lock on the pram. The sockeye run is fantastic this year.

7-18-1971 We are now on strike against P.N.B. Summer has

finally arrived. Grace is quite ill. We golfed again. Useless Bay now charges $3.00 green fees.

Wil was a lineman for the telephone company. P.N.B. is Pacific Northwest Bell which was eventually taken over by AT&T. The garage out front is filled with discarded wooden crossbeams and galvanized brackets that he would bring home from jobs. He had plans for them, I'm just not sure what they were.

8-29-1971 We are up on vacation. I came up by myself for the first 4 weekdays because Lucille had to work.

9-10-1971 Lucille caught two more Humpies during some rough weather. The wind was from the southeast. She used a white dodger and fresh Herring. Lucille is now ill with the flu or seasickness.

9-17-1971 We are babysitting Chris (grandson) this week. We brought him to Whidbey.

10-30-1971 Turned water off. Grace (Lucille's mother) passed away Oct. 27, '71, 6:10 PM.

2-13-1972 We had a huge amount of snow this winter - 16" to 2' on the ground. I was ill this winter with a severe cold in the chest. We foreclosed on the Millers. They left our little McMicken house in shambles. They were filthy, lazy tramps.

3-4-1972 Everything OK so far, although we had a terrific winter. I'm in the line gang at F.A.A. M.D. still isn't speaking to us, neither is Scott!

15 JOURNAL #2

This journal is the same size and dimension as #1, less than ¼ inch thick but standard notebook size or layout. It covers almost seven years, from June of 1972 to December of 1979. Lucille and Wil are now 48 years old, this log will take them into their mid-50's.

6-3-1972 Just finished 1st week of 1972 vacation. The weather was superb, 70-88 degrees with a lot of calm seas. Had heavy Chevy tuned after it failed us on the ferry dock. We now have new plugs and plug wires, points, rotor and condenser at 56,000 miles. Lucille beat me unmercifully at golf at Holmes Harbor.

6-17-1972 Mowed lawn. Am working at Bremerton. Lucille and M.D. are driving to Calif and left me holding the bag for Father's Day.

You will see that this is the first of many trips that Lucille and daughter (or other folks) will take together while Wil stays home. His statement about 'left holding the bag' tells me that he wasn't happy about it. As time goes by, he becomes very angry and resentful about being left home. I wonder what the real story is there? Does he not like to travel? Does she not want him along? Maybe he is miserable to travel with? I've known some folks like that and I would just as soon have left them home. This is the first of many clues that Wil resents others for his unhappiness and perhaps his loneliness. He believes that life is unfair to him. I wish he could see how that isolates him. I wish I could tell him that missed opportunities for togetherness are gone forever. I wish I could share the loneliness I felt during the latter part of my life after my husband left me. I was such a strong-willed person, I didn't need anybody. But the truth was that I did need somebody.

3-3-1973 Everything is A.OK. We had a beautiful February. First time up for Lucille this year.

5-5-1973 Put out anchor block with the aid of skin suit. Dug clams. The starfish are back. Quite windy today.

6-16-1973 Came up mowed yard. New renters in the Webster place. They used our buoy and went adrift in a storm. The ferry crew saved her. Our little dog Mooney died Friday.

9-30-1973 Mowed yard. Nice warm, calm day. Had leak in water valve under house. Lucille won a blue ribbon for her knitted stocking cap at the Puyallup Fair! M.D. & Scott have bought a new home in Mountainaire. They are flying to Baja this week.

10-14-1973 Vice President Agnew has resigned. We've been taking care of Chris the past couple weekends. It's been raining a little heavier lately.

11-10-1973 Came up to haul boat down. Lucille is trying out an L.T.D.

12-8-1973 Lucille bought the L.T.D.! Winterized lawn mower.

5-12-1974 Lucille & I are on vacation. Bob and family & Maridel and Chris came up. We had all kinds of bad weather - rain, lightning, hail, wind & even an earthquake! Lucille dominated the golfing scene.

6-16-1974 M.D., Scott and Chris came up for Fathers Day. Terrific weather. I received a new golf bag, slacks and gardening book.

5-11-1975 Ed passed away in his sleep a week ago. It's going to be awful lonely up here without Ed. He was a wonderful friend. The weather has been bad the past couple weekends, rainy & windy.

I'll miss Ed too. They had a little cabin just down the road from Wil's. Ed and Wil got along somehow. You know, that goes to show you that there are all sorts of folks around and even if you are not the easiest kind of person to get along with, there is someone who finds you A-OK.

7-20-1975 Caught a trout on a squid. Saw the air show from our place, really great. Our Skagit is still anchored out! Bonnie is getting store bought teeth this summer.

10-4-1975 Mowed. Silver and Humpie fishing are closed. Pushed logs off beach. Carol is going to become a Catholic.

11-16-1975 Mick had a slide behind her place. They are burying another telephone cable down our road. Lucille is supposed to be riding the hydrofoil between Hawaii and Honolulu today! Neighbors had a couple windows broken around Halloween time.

12-6-1975 Tremendous rainfall caused quick snow melt and flooded Ore. & Wash. $50 million damage in King and Snohomish County. Scott & M.D. are on their way back from a Honduras vacation by small plane.

12-27-1975 Everything OK after 70 M.P.H. wind gusts with 12' tides. Lucille has quit traveling long enough to come up with me this weekend.

3-7-1976 Sand lowest in years. Walked over. We have purchased a motorcycle. Yamaha 250! Scott flew to L.A. to see about a different job this week.

3-28-1976 Somebody has tried to jimmy our bedroom window! They also jimmied our neighbors.

4-3-1976 Now we've got a broken water pipe at east edge of meter box. The ferry fare for car/driver and passenger round trip is $4.90!

5-2-1976 There are still a lot of thefts along our beach. We now have a new watchdog named Bunny. She is 7 weeks old. Lucille has had a bad cold for a week and a half.

5-9-1976 Mowed. Cleaned bird nests out of attic with three eggs involved, what a mess. Lucille has had a bad cough for three weeks!

5-16-1976 Lucille made it to another birthday. We golfed Saturday and dug some nice clams on a -2.5 tide. Water pipe still not fixed.

5-31-1976 Am on vacation. Weather rainy and cold. Lucille is recovering from a bumped nose after running into the Kent sliding glass door.

10-22-1976 Mowed. Issacs got another German Sheppard. We can't believe it. We're sure disappointed in them. Foggy & calm weather.

11-7-1976 Turned off water. Am working 6 days a week, nine hours per day. Lucille is ill with bad cough.

2-26-1977 Had a marvelous vacation in Hawaii. Winter very dry. Skiing almost unheard of.

4-30-1977 Still haven't put out buoy. A bird got in our cabin, laid an egg and raised havoc, finally dying.

7-9-1977 Not coming up very often this year. Working a lot of Saturdays. Lucille's relatives swarmed in on us all at the same time at Kent over the 4th. Harold's boy was in a bad auto accident this week.

Well there, she does have some relatives, but Wil never names them, not that I can figure out.

7-17-1977 Two Canadian jets crashed into Puget Sound during the air show. Both pilots ejected and parachuted OK. Scrubbed our buoy.

8-14-1977 Still haven't launched Skagit! A very hot July & August. 22 days without rain, 18 days over 80 degrees, 5 days over 90 degrees. Neighbors have big dogs. Everything is tinder dry, people are running out of water.

10-2-1977 Mowed. Brought our grandson, Chris, up to help rake. Lucille went to his soccer game yesterday. His is on a 6 yr. old team. The Indian fishing controversy still rages on. The Sound is closed to non-Indian commercial fishing this week. I didn't catch a Salmon this year - first time since '46.

If you're not from around here you might not know what a hullaballoo was created with the enforcement of long-time laws governing Indian fishing rights. The local folks have to abide by the WA State Fishing laws while the Tribal folks only have to abide by their Tribal laws. This right to fish and hunt was granted to them in the late 1800's when they signed treaties with the US. Many folks who make their livin' on fishing were pretty mad about it all. It got downright dangerous out there. Fishermen who didn't pay heed to the law and went out anyway were turning up missing - their boats would be found floating empty. Now mind you I only know of one for real sure, but I did hear about several others. Things have calmed down over the years, but you can still hear the local island folk grumbling about the fishing or crabbing during the season and how unfair the laws are to them. They also complain about the commercial fishermen and they aren't Indian. I think they just need something to complain about when they aren't catching anything or maybe just need something to complain about period. I don't care about it one whit and besides, most years there is plenty fish and crab to be caught.

10-16-1977 The County has built up the road behind us! Our garage is now useless! We can't believe how they have ruined people's property along this road! Beautiful weather, we stayed overnight, we changed our buoy.

11-26-1977 Walked over. The sand has returned, we gained a couple feet. Some people are petitioning against the new road work! They want the road lowered.

12-17-1977 Lucille and I came up to check things out. Our little cabin has just survived a 14.6 tide with rough water included! It looks like the tide came to our second course of shingles on the skirting of the cabin. Several counties have been declared a disaster area. The heavy rains have caused millions in damage.

2-11-1978 Lucille bought a new Kitchen Aid dishwasher for Valentine's Day. Scott and M.D. returned from Costa Rica Friday. Roy has been ill for 2 weeks. Some logs left our beach in exchange for some different and longer ones.

4-30-1978 Lucille and Leta returned from Hawaii a week ago. Mowed. Sunny today for a change. Lots of Navy ships out today.

6-3-1978 Lucille is in two tournaments bowling this week end. I'm up here mowing and trim painting. We had record heat today 86 degrees. Everett had a celebration and put on a beautiful fireworks display at about 10:00 PM.

6-16-1978 We have a 36 yd pile of dirt in our yard. Roy Young made all the arrangements and the dump trucks came through his yard. M.D., Scott and Chris came up for Fathers' Day! Received a nice water jug, Hibachi and a riding lawnmower!

5-26-1979 Memorial Day weekend. Lucille now has a Thunderbird '77 model and gave it a first ferry ride today. Gas is very scarce. None of the South Whidbey stations are open. The weather has been miserable this weekend. Lightning and thunder with hail and heavy rain. We managed to play nine at Useless Bay, $5.50 each. Roy has started an oyster farm. Lucille burned her finger, has hay fever, blistered heel and a tired shoulder from packing her clubs.

I remember there were two gas shortages over the past ten years. The first one in 1973 and this one in 1979. The lines for gasoline were very long, tempers high and prices through the roof. I'm glad I'm not around for all this nonsense - some Arab countries controlling the price of the gas we buy. This would have cut into my profits operating the ferry line and I would have been hoppin mad I can tell you! I just don't understand it all.

6-13-1979 Gas is still scarce, price is 91 cents per gallon. Lucille fell asleep and sunburned her face and squeezed her finger on the tailgate.

8-23-1979 Foggy this morning. Lucille knocked them dead again this morning with 2 oz of lead and her half and half dodger. Outgoing Tide. She caught a 6 lb. Humpie at 7:30 am at the pink house.

9-9-1979 Seafair Derby this weekend. Roy says a local kid caught a 32 lb King at the pink house. Lucille collapsed last Thursday morning! Looks like Whidbey power has been off for ½ hour this past week.

9-14-1979 Lucille is gradually recovering, she was well enough to net a nice 9 lb. Silver that I hooked at noon!

9-17-1979 Commercial boats have moved in thicker than fleas. We fish from Jim Johns to Hat Island and old Clinton and never got a bump!

12-19-1979 We had over 1" of snow last weekend. Gas is over $1.00 per gallon. U.S. is trying to get back hostages from Iran. Tacked gutter back on and raked leaves.

16 JOURNAL #3

This is the first of two much thicker journals - spiral-bound, 8.5 x 11" format but about 1' thick. This one covers eleven years, from March of 1980 to January of 1991. Wil was much "wordier" in this journal. Wil and Lucille were in their mid-50's to later 60's during the time of this writing.

3-30-1980 Nice day at last! Mt. St. Helens erupted last week! Maple Valley had a tornado yesterday plus hail as big as golf balls. Our temporary buoy is missing again. Only two ferries are available due to the Hood Canal bridge sinking and the Vashon is damaged.

There! I thought it was a mistake to build a bridge that floats. Now it sunk and how are folks going to get across the Hood Canal? My little ferry would have taken them. Yes there were a few times that I didn't feel like making the run, but overall, I was reliable. You know, when I died they spread my ashes over that stretch of water where I operated my last ferry run - the Hood Canal route. Some say my ghost had something to do with it sinking - you don't believe that do you?

5-18-1980 Used our Stihl chain saw to cut thru stumps and logs resting on our ramp. Since Ed is gone nobody pushes the logs off in the winter anymore. Golfed twice at Useless. Their price has gone up to $5.50 for 9 holes on the weekend. Mt. St. Helens erupted at 8:30 A.M. this Sunday. We thought it was a sonic boom. We were lucky to have a north wind. The ash went south and east! Ferry fare is now $6.90 round trip car and passenger.

11-1-1980 Took Friday off sick. Very rainy & windy Saturday. The sailboats raced around Hat Island, beautiful sight during the storm. Lucille & I ate at the Admirals Mistress to celebrate our 34th anniversary.

2-8-1981 Walked over. President Reagan has deregulated gas prices. Regular jumped 10 cents a gallon to $1.26. Refrigerator still runs all the time. Lucille thinks she broke her little toe kicking the furniture a week ago. M.D. & Scott returned from Costa Rica last week.

2-23-1981 Lucille drove to Portland with M.D.. She put about 350 miles on the T-Bird. Her toe still hurts quite a bit. We had a very bad windstorm during the week at 3:00 A.M. The new computerized ferries (Issaquah, etc.) are tied up as unsafe!

4-15-1981 The space men just returned to earth on the Columbia. New ferries are still tied up as unsafe. The 51 year old Vashon has been taken out of service. I replaced 8 shingles on the roof.

This is another activity that amazed me to watch! This 6'3" man climbing up a ladder to put a few shingles into place on the roof. He continues to do this into his 80's! When I think about it, I guess that would have been me too. Why hire someone to do something when you can do it yourself? And look at all the trouble they are having with these new-fangled ferry boats! Things were simpler in the day I ran a ferry.

5-30-1981 Lucille returned from Hawaii last Saturday. We mowed for the first time in a month! They have taken the new ferries off our run. They can't land on extreme high or low tides. Saturday we saw a man catch a salmon over 10lb. right out in front of our place. He appeared to be trolling without a dodger.

6-5-1981 Took a day-at-a-time vacation Friday. Lucille & I golfed at Useless on the back nine. We are back to 3 old ferries. Lucille rowed me around in the rain for ½ hour. I had two strikes.

I'd watch that woman, Lucille, as she would go out with Wil fishing. He would sit there for an hour or more rigging up his rod and getting ready to fish while she sat so patiently. Then she would row him around so that he could troll. Now that is dedication or patience or love or something!

6-20-1981 Came up for Father's Day. Lucille rowed out and picked up a Styrofoam block. I followed suit later in the day. Several mountain climbers were covered with an avalanche on

93

Fathers Day at Mt. Rainier.

8-17-1981 Monday we went up to Nick's Appliance an ordered a new 1981 15 cubic foot G.E. refrigerator. $579.00!

8-20-1981 Lucille finally caught an 8 lb. Humpy with her squid! It almost pulled her in! She caught her hood string in her reel handle and couldn't pay out line!

8-21-1981 Lucille did it again! She caught a beautiful 5 lb. Silver on her squid & 6oz. North wind, 10:50 A.M. in front of Taylors, 1 hr. after high tide change.

9-14-1981 Last Friday the phone company gave me a beautiful cake, wristwatch and belt buckle for 35 years of outstanding service.

9-16-1981 My 35th P.N.B. anniversary. Lucille left her glasses ashore. Lucille couldn't even see to bait her hook without her glasses. She then proceeded to catch her limit right in front of the cabin. Her catch included a 30 lb. King! The Groesbecks came over to find out just how Lucille fishes!

10-24-1981 Came up in T-Bird with Keith. Beautiful weather. Mowed. Lucille is back from Puerta Vallarta Mexico last week. World Series is on - N.Y. & L.A.

11-21-1981 Last weekend we had a terrific wind & rain storm. It knocked down 7 million board feet of timber. The storm tipped over a sailboat off Hat Island with 60 m.p.h. winds. The 31 year old Mr. Taylor from Taylor's Landing and another man drowned.

12-6-1981 Walked over with Lucille and Bunny. Lucille turned off refrigerator and unplugged it. Ole Manz and his neighbors had their homes burglarized last month. They took rifles, spotting scopes, washing machines, etc.

1-30-1982 Stayed overnight but did not turn water on. Very stormy after I got up here so stayed over, using bedspreads for covers. 50 degrees in the cabin this morning.

3-27-1982 Came up from Edmonds by myself. Lucille is quite upset with me. All I wanted to do was protect her from working too hard because of all her relatives barging in on us. So I get blamed! Mowed yard with Firestone and weed eater.

4-24-1982 They lost a car off the ferry Cathlamet on 4-21-82. The captain had the rudder in the wrong position, the ferry drifted far enough to have a gap between ferry and dock and the car dropped in the water. Lucille is back in Washington D.C. again! She left Friday with Dee and Don. I'm stuck home taking care of cat & dog.

5-15-1982 Mowed. Weed eater cord burned up just as I finished. The birds are back in the cabin again. Lucille is traveling again! She has been gone for a week driving to California with Leta.

5-22-1982 Lucille returned from west coast trip. Turned on hot water tank. Painted south wall of guest room with Olympic overcoat. We golfed at Holmes Harbor, Useless Bay has now been closed to the public since last July.

6-19-1982 Came up for weekend and 3 days vacation using day-at-a-time. Lucille gave me a 2 h.p. Johnson Sea Horse for Fathers' Day! I waxed it with Turtle wax. Lucille couldn't stay up on my 3 day vacation, she had to work because her boss is in Norway for 3 weeks.

6-26-1982 We cut some logs that blocked our ramp using our Stihl 041 and the new "come along". That little dickens pulls quite a load.

10-30-1982 Mowed. A ship burned and sank 2 weeks ago in Everett harbor. A purse seiner sank during a windstorm in Saratoga Passage. Lucille returned from Mexico last Sunday at 6:45 p.m.

11-22-1982 I am now as old as Lucille - 59! Supposed to be colder than 27 degrees tonight so I am draining the pipes.

1-15-1983 Sand is higher than in years. We also have a lot of logs out front. My leg aches something fierce.

1-29-1983 Walked over. Hundreds of logs drifting around. My leg has ached since Sept. 82.

2-20-1983 Walked over. Leg is feeling much better, at least I can sleep at night now. We've got tons of logs out front and on the ramp. 13 Chinese were executed at a Seattle gambling joint over this Washington B.D. (birthday) weekend.

3-6-1983 We have a ton of logs out front. I am trying to cut my way out. Roy Young had a detached retina last week. He is just back from the hospital today. Couldn't get the oil stove started. Flat calm this weekend.

3-20-1983 I still have the big timber on the ramp. Used oil stove again. Two people were murdered at Langley last week.

5-15-1983 Lucille got a G.E. toaster for her birthday. Still haven't put the permanent anchor out. Had an ingrown hair on my chest. Lucille dug a big batch of clams.

5-30-1983 We found a 16' and 20' 2x4 on our beach. Lucille wouldn't go get them in her house coat. Everybody and his dog was up here this weekend.

7-17-1983 Some fog Saturday morning. Air show at Paine Field today. The SR71 spy plane was on display. Maridel left for Peru on Saturday.

8-21-1983 Lucille caught 2 Shakers with a pink buzz bomb and 6 oz. We are still on strike against P.N.B.! I picketed Wed. Aug. 17, 1983 2:00 to 5:30p.m.

8-22-1983 P.N.B. strike settled with A.T. & T. except for local issues. We are not back to work yet.

8-27-1983 We've been using up all of our bait every day! Lucille lost her favorite two tone dodger. I didn't re-tie the knot in time. Seafair Derby is this weekend. Pretty crowded up here.

8-28-1983 Earthquake this morning at 5:45 a.m.

10-30-1983 Still mowing the yard! Lucille and Maridel came back from Mexico last Wednesday. Hurricane Tico went thru Mazatlan and Puerto Vallarta while they were there.

1-17-1984 Retired as of Jan 1, 1984!!!! Lucille is still working! Weather is cool & clean. Scenery is beautiful. Retired life is lonesome.

Wil is 60 years old now and he is retired. He has always worked, often overtime, and he doesn't have a world outside of work except the cottage. No wonder he is lonesome. Lucille probably still wants to work. I didn't have that problem. I always worked and after my divorce in 1936 I never re-married. So I was alone for the last 20 years of my life. Of course I had my kids, but they get busy, you know how it is.

3-5-1984 The Navy is thinking about moving a task force to Everett, that will finish off our fishing. The game department is talking about closing the ocean and Sound to all fishing due to the effects of "El Nino" a warming of ocean waters.

4-17-1984 The Navy has chosen Everett for its home port. Everything is going downhill around here. There are sea lions out front and I saw an eagle today. Lucille bought a new L.T.D. Crown Victoria with everything on it! Looks like the charter parasites are fishing up in front of our house because their normal area is closed. What next!?

Oh there he goes, he really hates those commercial fishermen and charter fishing boats. Somehow Wil thinks the water in front of his cottage is his personal fishing space and the beach is his own beach. I guess he isn't alone in that thinking, but it sure isn't good for your health to think that way.

4-29-1984 We now have to have a Coast Guard sticker and a state sticker on all size boats with motors. Another $10.00 for the rotten parasites.

5-15-1984 Lucille is now 61 years of age! I came up to hang her new window blind in the kitchen. I also dove (at 60 years of age) for the anchor line, it's been on the bottom since last November.

6-22-1984 70 degrees after an 1 ½" of rain a couple days ago.

Lucille is in Hawaii with Chris. She is at Sea Mountain on the Big Island after being on the Kona Coast for a week.

6-30-1984 Mowed. Still having a problem with those miserable builders working on house next door. They are throwing lots of nails in our lawn and on our roof! Lucille and Chris just got back from Hawaii. Lucille walked out in her shorts and tennis shoes to hook up new buoy line. We brought up my new 5" Hitachi T.V. portable. It works fine on rabbit ears.

The house that belonged to Inga has been torn down and is being replaced by a new 3-story monstrosity. Wil is not happy about it and I don't blame him one bit! The house will eventually block the sunshine from shining on the little wooden cottage during much of the year. It is being built just 5 feet from the property line next to Wil's and just looms over the little cottage. A sign of the times to come - eventually this beach will see many more new, overly-big homes where small fishing cabins once stood. The whole neighborhood will change and I'm not sure for the better.

Little cottage dwarfed by new homes on each side

7-11-1984 That old electrician in the Econoline is down here and the masonry man. They were digging our clams and didn't cover the holes. I reminded them of the nail problem. Lucille collapsed at work yesterday! Lucille just got back from Hawaii then she went to Nampa, Idaho for Jeffs wedding. I guess it was just too much traveling for her.

7-21-1984 Came up with Lucille. Builders are still working on house next door. Our 6' stepladder has been stolen! We don't know whether it's one of these builders or the nerds to the north of us who are always having garage sales. They've got Dianes house looking like a garbage dump!

So Diane is the nice lady who owns the house north of Wil. For many years, she just rents it out and doesn't live there. She bought it from Captain Melling - another ferry captain and relation of mine who was around these parts a long time. A great cabin, but eventually Diane gets married and she and her new husband Jim tear down that lovely old cabin and build another one of those overly-big homes in the place where that cabin sat. It sat right next to the garage that belonged to Wil. I was real sad to see that cabin gone, it was part of the fishing cabin era now long-gone on Whidbey.

8-20-1984 Launched the Skagit at last! The builders are through at Jims. They still have not restored our yard! We had to shovel the sand off the ramp at Langley, nobody has done anything about it since last year! Lucille went to Mason lake. She slept outside.

9-15-1984 I had nice calm, warm weather during the past couple of weeks. I only had to bail 4 buckets out of Skagit. The commercial fishermen are thick on the Sound. The young man renting Diane's house hasn't found a job for months.

9-25-1984 Back up fishing again, this retirement is great! Somebody has tied a plastic bottle to my anchor chain! I scoured the buoy, and discovered it. Some fool started a fire in a huge pile of tires near Everett. The fire department poured a million gallons of water on it to no avail. The water started to pollute the Snohomish River so they quit. They are going to let the fire take its own course.

10-11-1984 Came up to pull anchor buoy. Too rainy and windy. Tire fire still going. Front door was not latched. Used oil stove again.

11-11-1984 Lucille finally stopped traveling and came up to Whidbey with me! She hasn't been up for 2 months! We pulled our blue anchor buoy and put out a temporary using a 5/16 full threaded bolt. We have gained sand half way up our ramp! The result of an early storm. Bunny has been blind for a couple months.

12-26-1984 The F.B.I. burned a white supremacist to death up at Freeland a few weeks ago. It took about 100 agents to do the job. They closed the shipping channel on the west side. We had a beautiful Christmas at Maridels. Scott didn't show up. We've had a terrible oil spill from Mukilteo-Clinton line to Scatchet Head. Hundreds of birds became oil soaked and died. Officials estimate the amount of sludge and oil to be 5,000 gallons! The perpetrators should get 10 years in jail and a fine! We've also had a couple mudslides. One behind us and a worse one behind Monohans. Their house is splattered up to the roof and his driveway is full of mud & stumps. Our garage gate blew off its' hinges. Other than that, all is fine. Mr. Young is now retired.

1-26-1985 Beach oil pretty well gone. Dry winter, some fog and 32 degree temps. Lucille is going to Hong Kong next week.

2-23-1985 Lucille and M.D. returned from Hong Kong last Monday. Things look OK over here on Whidbey. The F.B.I. arrested a bunch of bandito drug & gun runners up at Bellingham this week.

3-13-1985 I guess those crab pots are not Olson's. Some commercial parasite is setting them out! The vessel's name is Native Sky out of Bellingham! Yard needs mowing but I have a cold. Lucille brought me a cold back from Hong Kong. I've been retired 1 yr and 2 months.

5-1-1985 Lucille is thinking about quitting work in a couple of weeks. The winter ducks are still here and so are the sea lions. There is another offshore drilling rig being refurbished at Everett.

5-7-1985 Lucille has fired 3 prospective replacement bookkeepers. Her bookkeeping methods are so old fashioned, they are unable to grasp it. At the rate she is going, she will not retire on May 15th.

5-18-1985 Lucille came up for the first time since 11-11-84. There are a lot of sports fishermen out this weekend. Our temporary buoy is missing! It was OK 2 weeks ago! Lucille is now 62 years of age! She had a wonderful birthday with lots of gifts and cards at work. Mt. St. Helens blew 5 years ago. Bathroom sink hot water pipe under sink had to have a new washer.

6-4-1985 Lucille dug clams today. The winter oil spill didn't hurt them. It was stormy and rainy this morning.

6-17-1985 Lucille is retired sort of! She had a retirement banquet at the Golden Steer then she worked one more day. We came up Monday evening and stayed Tuesday. The weather is marvelous. M.D. is going to Mexico with Chris and their Peruvian exchange student.

7-1-1985 Maridel & Chris have returned from Mexico. Lucille & I had to wait 7 hours at the airport on Lucille's retirement party night! All I got was 1 shot of Whiskey and no cake because of that airport fiasco!

7-16-1985 Ken thinks he had a slight heart attach down at Treasure Island. He is undergoing tests. Ken's house was burglarized. I was up here at the time. Lucille is still training her replacement!

8-5-1985 Mr. Young has gone back to work for a new company. Diane's house is empty. Jim's relatives from S. Dakota have just showed up, never any privacy around here! Maridel got her Volvo out of the garage last Friday. They couldn't even fix it!

8-15-1985 Lucille has retired again. The weather has turned hot 85-90 degrees. She finally came up again for a few days. After the tide change we caught Shakers on Lucille's buzz bomb and 6 oz.

8-23-1985 Les passed away last week. He just sold the Columbia Beach Resort and moved up on Humphrey Road. He was 72 years old. We finally took the rug that used to be in Maridel's house outside and trimmed some off the edge. We plan to lay it in the front room.

8-26-1985 We finally hit the jackpot! I shortened our strip rig leaders to 24" and caught a 10 lb. Humpie at 7:30 am. Also caught a 5 lb Silver at 8:15 am. We caught all the fish in front of Jim-John's. I had another big one on and almost up to the boat. After I lost it I reeled in the line and was just going to bring the bait over the side when a big salmon raced up to the edge of the boat, thrashed at the bait, missed, but splashed Lucille in the face! The miserable commercial fisherman are in here already! Both seiners and gillnetters are fishing the Mukilteo side already!

9-21-1985 Lucille has had an upset stomach so she hasn't been going out fishing. She finally went out. We used up our gas so she had to row in. While she rowed I fished just to ferry dock without any weight at all. Mr. Young has the flu. Bob bought a camper, it used to belong to Les before he passed away.

10-30-1985 Lucille just got back from a 4,000 mile auto trip. She and Leta traveled around Oregon, Utah, Nevada, Arizona and California. She drove our new Crown Victoria L.T.D. The commercial crybabies are still fishing down in Hood's Canal! It's been their best year in 20 years!

11-7-1985 Snow is forecast so I came up to drain pipes. I pumped out Skagit and put on tarp. Roy says there are some otters on our beaches.

12-10-1985 We had one of the worst snow storms since 1896. As soon as we had the snow the temperature dipped below freezing and the snow remained just as it had fallen for 2 weeks. Oil tanker spilled 200,000 gallons of crude oil from Alaska at Port Angeles at Christmas time.

2-7-1986 The oil drilling platforms have not left Everett or Hat Island yet. They were being retrofitted. Our permanent buoy was left out all winter. Lucille is still working so I get very little help. Leta passed away on Feb. 18, 1986.

4-8-1986 Sea lions are thick up here. They are eating a lot of Salmon. 71 degrees today. Lucille is still working. Cats are trying to take over the beach. LeeRoy Young is trying to fence them out. The Starlings are also plaguing us.

4-29-1986 Sea lions are still around eating Salmon. There is supposed to be 700 of them in the area. The lady in Diane's house has a new lawnmower and she is grooming the lawn nicely. The Russians have had a nuke power plant fire at Kiev. Lucille is still working.

5-27-1986 Bob is now retired after 41 yrs and 35 days of line work. Lucille also retired on May 14. Lucille is 63 years old! We have been here for 6 days for a long Memorial Day weekend since Lucille is now retired.

Well I know that Wil is very hopeful that long stays at the cottage will now be a part of the retirement program for he and Lucille. Not in the cards from what I can see (and I can see quite a lot from my view-point).

6-22-1986 The caterpillars are thick this summer. Came up by myself to work on anchor buoy as Lucille left for Puerto Vallarta Mexico on June 13. Nothing has changed since she retired on May 14. She still thinks it's great to leave me home alone. I got an on sale weed-eater for Father's Day from Jafco-Best. Felix is acting quite weird in her old age. They are working on the ferry dock, the ferry ran into it again. Les has sold his house and bought a big boat. Our taxes on the cabin have come down a little since they built the big house to the south of us. Our water pipe has been repaired. There are 248 cases of AIDS in Washington State.

7-7-1986 Finally Lucille has come up to Whidbey. Mowed lawn with the old moto mower. LeeRoy and Bob both have sea gull chasers on their boats now. The local people had a lot of thefts from their moored boats! Bob lost binoculars & an air horn. Someone lost reels and Mr. Robinson lost 5 poles and reels. Some parasites are trying to start aquaculture pens in the Sound. The people are up in arms about it. They are unsightly and polluting. A 56 lb. King was caught here last week! The largest King ever checked in to McConnells. The man was using a green squid 100 feet deep and a down rigger. Elliott Bay will be closed Aug 1 to protect the King run.

9-10-1986 The purse seiners were in for one day. We thought they cleaned everything out but fishing the next day has been OK. All the commercials are jamming Shilshole Bay this week.

9-20-1986 The otter left a foot long Sole in the back of our boat near the motor. The weather has been flat calm. Bud who lives near the Schultzes had his dinghy stolen from his yard on the weekend. His neighbor had a motor stolen around the end of August. The ferry Cathlamet hit the Clinton ferry dock again. This time it is going to cost about 1 million dollars to fix! The crash happened on Sept. 12. They brought the Cathlamet back on the 14th and 21st but it still is not right so they have gone back to the drawing board. For a while we were down to 1 ferry and the commuter line up was 3 hours long. The commercial parasites are really thick at Edmonds, Possession and Mukilteo. They are even delaying the Edmonds ferry.

10-3-1986 Felix has a bladder problem this year. Quite foggy. Commercial fishermen clogging the Sound. One gillnetter lost his net to the ferry "Evergreen State" in the fog.

10-7-1986 The county is cleaning the ditch, we glommed onto some Alder off the bank for firewood. Felix passed away today.

10-29-1986 Our roof on the east portion leaked a little after that long dry spell. Lucille walks to the store to improve her wind. Brought up the Firestone mower. Still mowing at this time of year. Commercial bums are still fishing up here.

11-8-1986 It is supposed to get down in the twenties tonight, so I am draining the pipes.

Wil is pretty faithful about draining the pipes so they don't freeze and burst when it gets really cold. He even drains the water heater! Once he has drained all the water out, he doesn't turn it back on until he is sure there will be no more freezing - sometime late in spring. That's why you won't see very many journal entries between November and May - just too cold to turn the water on. Coming up to the cottage while the water is turned off is not very convenient. Now I didn't have all the plumbing fixtures that he has but that was in the 20's and this is now the 80's!

12-31-1986 Came over to check logs. We are expecting higher than normal tides. Everything OK so far. Sunny day today. Lucille is in London.

1-13-1987 Lucille is back from Europe. Ned and Sandy are arguing. Super high tides caused by the moon, sun and earth aligning. It uprooted our protecting stump and dumped our cedar log behind the buffer bulkhead. Roy has tied another big log in front of our place. He does keep an eye on our place though.

1-30-1987 I have been up here for three days, getting up at 4:30 and 5:00 AM checking rough weather and tide logs. I used my waders in the morning darkness to push some troublesome big logs away just as they were starting to end up in front of our place. Those waders and pike pole paid for themselves. I had to turn the water back on.

2-8-1987 A real bad storm came in on Jan 31. Wind and high (13.2) tides. During the high water, Mr. Young pushed away a troublesome stump and a log that I had been cutting on (3' in diameter). That was a load off my mind.

3-22-1987 Mowed tall grass for the first time this year. Came over alone. Bob mowed his too. Lucille flew to Reno.

4-9-1987 Mowed again. Turned on water, did not fill hot water tank.

5-9-1987 We saw the replica of Capt. Vancouver's rowing dory sailing down the Sound. We also drove up to Langley to see a new stern wheeler which was built by Nichols Boat Works for use in Alaska. It's called the Discovery III.

5-14-1987 Lucille had her 64th birthday on Whidbey. Lucille dug clams on a -3.5 tide. I scrubbed our temporary buoy. The sea gulls have been pecking at it! Used my waders to reach it on a calm -3.3 tide. We mowed with the old silent mower, it could be sharper.

7-13-1987 The ferries are using the south slip again and they didn't learn much after wrecking the dock to the tune of $500,000, they are coming in fast and making huge waves on our bulkhead. Lucille dug some nice clams on a -3.7 tide. I finally tried my new Penn 209 reel. Had one strike. The small swivel broke in the middle on my strip rig leader.

8-13-1987 I caught a 6 lb Silver and a 6 lb Humpie. Lucille gave me a new Penn 209 to do the trick. They are having good luck with squids for the Humpies especially pink colors and a white dodger.

8-28-1987 The summer has been so sunny and dry we are having water rationing in Seattle and Bellevue. I've had my second root canal at my dentist. The second one made my face swell up and he's put me on penicillin. Everybody on the beach have put wheels on their smaller boats - Gene, LeeRoy, Jim and Bob.

9-5-1987 We still haven't had any rain. I caught a nice 8 lb Humpie. Lucille threw back a 17" Blackmouth. It is the driest since 1919. We have forest fires all up and down the coast. It's about 80 degrees every day. The penicillin helped my tooth and the doctor finished my right side root canal last Tuesday. Our apples in Kent are the largest we've ever had.

9-12-1987 Dr. Weitz is still working on my two bum teeth. Last week I was in for a 1.5 hr appointment. I retrieved Bob's aluminum boat. His knot must have worked loose. June thanked us. Lucille saw it get away.

9-25-1987 Dr. Weitz finally finished restoring my two teeth. He just finished when the power went off. The N.F.L. is on strike. We don't know what to do for entertainment

10-3-1987 Still having superb weather! 80 degrees! I mowed with silent mower. Pumped boat and put on tarp. Commercial bums are swarming all over the Sound. Dr. Weitz put a notch in one of my teeth. We are still having a drought.

10-12-1987 Came up on Columbus Day. Commercial bums are clogging the Sound. Dr. Weitz quickly fit the partial plate framework then went to lunch. Mr. Young put his big boat up for sale. Nobody has enough money to buy it. Lucille had a reunion with the Old Homemakers Club.

10-24-1987 Started Moto mower. Another trace of rain. The dentist finished my dental work! The stock market crashed 508 points on Black Monday. A pod of Blackfish went by today heading north. I put some more temporary asphalt wedges on the east roof and puttied the guest room window. The commercial boys are still clogging the Sound. Chris went to his high school homecoming, wearing a tuxedo this weekend.

11-17-1987 Commercial parasites are still fishing around here. Two Island County Sheriffs were slain by some Clinton degenerate last Saturday. Lucille has left me alone again. She has gone on another ridiculous trip to Hong Kong for a week starting Nov. 14. Returning Nov 22. She wasn't even home on my birthday and Maridel wasn't home on Chris's . That really hurts.

12-13-1987 Stayed up 3 days. I didn't close valve to hot water tank, so it filled up again. Lucille had to carry 52 gallons of water to the ditch. Mr. Young has decorated his flagpole with Christmas lights.

12-28-1987 The ferry Kittitas hit the Columbia Beach Dock again! They broke the wing wall! The weather was calm and the atmospheric pressure was high during the high tides so the water didn't get too high. Sawed logs and shoveled sand between bulkhead.

Well doggone it! What kind of folks do they have runnin those ferries? I hear one of their captains is known as "Captain Crunch" - now that's tellin a tale!

2-18-1988 South ferry slip at Columbia Beach is still out of commission. We are still behind in rainfall. The reservoirs are not up to par.

3-17-1988 I'm having trouble starting the Firestone mower. It's only 35 yrs old. The ferries are using the south slip again. Turned on cold water for the first time this year. There are 90 Grebe like birds out front.

4-8-1988 Got Firestone started, mowed Whidbey. Emptied roof bucket, it was full. Saw a flock of Goldeneye birds swim by. Bob has his place up for sale again. The mountains are beautiful after some heavy snowfalls. Started oil stove.

5-18-1988 Lucille is now a senior citizen. Our beach is really changing. A large sand spit is moving up from the south.

6-1-1988 Lucille dug some clams on a -3.2 tide. Rippees are divorcing and selling their place up near Goughs. Louis is recovering from his quadruple heart bypass surgery. He was in Swedish Hospital for a week.

6-22-1988 Chris has graduated from high school. We mowed. Lucille is just back after a week in Mexico!! Rippee's place has sold already for $150,000!

7-11-1988 Came up alone & mowed. Lucille is helping Maridel move northeast of Issaquah. Rained the day after I mowed. Louis is already back to work after his heart operation. LeeRoy Young bought another boat! It's an 18' aluminum I/O, 120 H.P. Starcraft. Lucille and I removed the living room rug and cut it up in one foot squares. The pink house burned down around the 4th of July.

8-3-1988 We've bought some dinghy wheels. They are the Easy Launch brand. Made in Lynnwood. $175.00 with tax! We just had a couple more 90 degree days. There has been some more outboard motor thefts. They took Gene's gas can and almost got his new motor but it was locked on.

8-18-1988 We finally laid the rug that Maridel gave us. We still have to trim it. We did some more mortaring on the bulkhead. Mr.

young's new boat has turned out to be a lemon. The engine is shot and the outdrive is shot. Mr. Knowles from Everett had his large 25' boat stolen from its buoy. They took it to Everett and stripped the electronic gear. Chris is off to W.S.U. with a brand new foot locker, credit card and checking account.

8-29-1988 Somebody around here is stealing outboards and marine electronics like mad on moored boats! We mounted Lucille's "Easy Launch" wheels on the Olympian dinghy. The otters are really making a mess in our boat.

12-7-1988 Pearl Harbor Day. Foggy and drizzly. The 100' Cottonwood is still out front of our bulkhead. Filled ice trays in refrigerator.

1-12-1989 Very rough today, winds 35 mph out of the south. The 100' cottonwood is still on our beach and starting to bury itself. The mountains are majestic today. We had very heavy snowfall in the mountains. Snoqualmie ski areas were without power for a couple days. Maridel and Bob went to Mexico for Christmas. Chris got kicked out of W.S.U. He now goes to Bellevue C.C. They had a large drug bust on Whidbey yesterday. The jerks are growing marijuana over here.

2-26-1989 Emptied ¾ bucket of water from attic. Mr. Young put out a crab pot today. The contractor who wants to raise Dianes' house wants to come through our yard to bring in his beams. They haven't called us yet to get permission. A fiberglass tri-hull beat itself to pieces against a bulkhead down by Jim 'n' Johns Resort. Parts of it are scattered all along the beach in front of us.

3-12-1989 It's been a wet, windy, snowy winter and spring. A mudslide behind Leafs this morning has plugged the ditch and blocked one lane of Columbia Beach Drive. Chris is going to Bellevue C.C. and working at West Coast Specialties.

3-29-1989 Still having a lot of rain. Emptied bucket from the attic again. The house north of the Ulrich house at the end of the road was sawed in sections and moved away this winter. They are now building a 2 story house on that lot, starting from scratch. They didn't save a wall. The ferry had steering problems yesterday. It was out of service for a couple hours. There has been the largest oil spill in U.S. history up at Valdez Alaska. Tanker went aground.

4-4-1989 First sunny days in a month!! mowed with the Firestone mower, it started on the first pull. I turned on the water for the 1st time this year. I didn't fill the hot water tank yet. The sea lions are ruining the Steelhead run at the Ballard locks. They have been hauled away 200 miles but they find their way back.

4-13-1989 Mowed again. Lucille came up for the first time this year. We rolled the logs out away from our ramp with a peavey. Mr. Young's dog Pup-Pup passed away in December.

4-28-1989 Lucille is on another ridiculous trip. This time it's to Hawaii with Betty and "Put". I have to take care of everything by myself again, it's a lonesome life. I've got to go someplace where I'm appreciated. This just isn't working out. The toilet tank leaked at the spud pipe. It caused some tiles to come up. I mowed again.

I'm real sad to hear Wil talk like that. He has become pretty dissatisfied with his life and you know what? - he only has himself to blame for that. His being all cranky and mad will only make himself unhappier. I think he has expectations of his Lucille and of his life that he keeps to himself. Then he does nothing to help them happen, least of all talking about them with Lucille. This is not a good road to be walking down. Take it from me - you got to make your life what it is, nobody is going to do that for you. Dang! I wish I could tell Wil that.

5-6-1989 Lucille is back from Hawaii. She dug some nice clams on a -3.2 tide. I took the dinghy out using our new wheels. I scrubbed the temporary buoy and line. I put some duct tape on the toilet tank drain elbow. Bob had a garage sale on 5-6-89.

5-16-1989 Lucille has a bad cough and cold. She brought it back from her Hawaiian trip. I had to come up by myself again. She is now 66 years young.

6-23-1989 We came up and mowed and pushed off logs on the

high tide. Our beach has changed dramatically. We have a lot of logs and high tide doesn't come near our bulkhead because the sand has built up so much. Toot Young is now retired.

7-12-1989 Fished with the Johnson 2 for the first time this year. We caught 1 Shaker. We didn't go out till noon!

7-22-1989 We finally took the tarp off the Skagit. The new neighbors caught an 18 lb King at the Clam Shack by Jim & Johns early in the morning on plain Herring. Elmer passed away last week. He had been ill for quite a while with heart problems. Mr. Young gave us some nice steamer clams cooked Chinese style.

1959 Skagit as it looked in 2011

8-1-1989 We brought up the F-100 and launched the Skagit. We also took 2 cans to the transfer station for $3.63. My neighbors to the south are remodeling their new home already! They are enclosing the deck to make a sun room, so we have more carpenters hanging around. "Big Bird" (the long-legged bird) is back.

8-13-1989 I touched up the boat trailer with black gloss Derusto. We drove down to the new bait sales place at Glendale. One of the Richardson boys is supposed to be running it. They gave us about 6 dozen Herring for $2.00! They are the small Herring we haven't seen that size in years.

8-27-1989 Lucille had a lot of strikes on her white dodger. The builders are still working on Tasches sun porch. The state is still widening the road from the ferry landing to the post office and around the grocery store. The new owner of the brick house above us is chopping the trees off the bank behind Tasches (neighbor to south).

9-10-1989 Car thieves tried to steal our little Courier at the Kent park and ride while we were at the Mariner baseball game. The Kent police helped us put the ignition key wiring back together. They broke our vent window and stole some pliers. I mowed today for the first time in about a month. The weather has been great. 80 degrees and calm. The commercial parasites are starting to fish this week.

9-17-1989 I guess the commercial parasites swept the area in front of our place a couple of days before Labor Day. The fishing has been lousy ever since. There were purse seiners. We ate out at the new Clover Patch at Bayview. We had teriyaki chicken.

9-26-1989 On the last day of this visit we were anchored out. The otters trashed our boat on a calm moonlit night. They had been using Lindy's son's open boat. We still have a lot of logs and sandy beach.

10-17-1989 San Francisco had a huge earthquake. Hundreds were killed. I mowed with the Firestone mower. The commercial parasites are still fishing around here. The Youngs have gone to Hawaii. Lucille has gone to Mexico with M.L. and Tana.

11-4-1989 Came up alone in the F-100. We've been having heavy rain. I drained the hot water tank. Boeing machinists are still on strike! Lucille came back from Mexico. She has a cough again.

11-14-1989 Boeings is still on strike. We've been having heavy rains. All the northern rivers are flooded. A bridge washed out on the Nooksack river. The Navy is starting to dredge Everett Harbor for the carrier homeport. I drained the cold and shut off under house at the gate valve and put in anti-freeze.

11-30-1989 Nice sunny day. A bunch more logs have landed on our beach. The Tasche's house is so tall, it keeps our house in the shade even at midday!

12-14-1989 Jeff and his new wife Amy visited us from Eugene, Oregon. He was driving a Bronco II. He is unemployed! His wife of 2 years works for an employment agency.

1-6-1990 Lucille bought me a new Ranger truck for Christmas! I gave it its 1st ferry ride today. There are so many logs on our beach, I can't get the dinghy out. Chris F. got some new boots for skiing. They cost almost $300.00! We had to get a new water heater in Kent over the New Years' weekend. It cost about as much as Chris F.'s new boots.

1-18-1990 Came up with the "Ranger". We've had a big slide behind Monohans & Leafs. The bank slid during the big rain storm that flooded Chehalis.

2-11-1990 Came up with "Ranger", looks like I'm snowed in. I may have to use my four wheel drive to get home. I caught some rainwater to use the toilet.

2-22-1990 Came up in Ranger. This is the first sunny day we've had in a month. The house movers are starting to move Lindfors two houses. He gave them away. Dump fees are so high that giving them away is the cheapest way to go. I emptied 3" out of bucket in attic. Lindfors houses are moved - one to Clinton and one to Saratoga. We are still having mud slides along Columbia Beach Drive.

3-11-1990 Pat and Lori's house was hit by lightning last night. It melted their telephones, broke their water line, broke the inside pane of a double pane window! Ruined some appliances, ruined the neighbors computer.

3-29-1990 Brought up Lucilles Christmas gift. "Sauder"#612 utility cart for the microwave we got from Maridel & Bob. I started the old Firestone mower and mowed weeds again. I saw a sea lion out front again. I also saw an eagle perched on Mr. Youngs' spar pole! I cleared logs so we can get our dinghy out to sea. I washed the Olympian. I rode the bike along the Heggenes Road, it's beautiful up there in the springtime. The otters are still here. I saw 3 of them this morning.

4-15-1990 We just had a very poor Easter! No ham dinner and Lucille is having another mood swing, she hasn't talked since Jeff left (he was staying with us). I've been trying to impress on her relatives that they are killing her. She just tried to do too much! Maridel is one of the worst offenders, encouraging Lucille to take all her ridiculous trips. It takes Lucille months to recover from those trips! I get blamed for being hostile to these cruel people, but they are not the ones who have to take care of her! Mowed with the Firestone just in time because it rained very hard the night after I finished.

5-4-1990 Came up in Ranger. Mowed with Sears mower. Lucille has taken another ridiculous trip. She's left for Europe on 5-3-90.

5-19-1990 Lucille just returned from another ridiculous trip to Europe. She was gone over 2 weeks to Germany, Switzerland, Italy with Joy and M.D. I mowed with Sears mower, hauled up in Ranger. The volcano at St. Helens happened 10 years ago.

5-23-1990 Lucille came up for the first time this year! We found our anchor block on a -4.0 tide. I used the waders Lucille gave me to take care of the anchor work, they are a great help.

6-9-1990 Mowed with Firestone. Trimmed limbs on tree. Still having heavy rains. We can just about count the sunny days of the year on one hand. The Valley strawberries may rot.

7-12-1990 Mowed lawn with Firestone. We are having great weather - 80-90 all week. The ferry Chelan hit the dock at Orcas

Island a couple weeks ago. They have brought her down, repaired her and are using her on our run.

7-27-1990 We drove to Lake Stevens and bought 3 squares of shingles from Pugsley Cedar Products for $80.00 per square. The weather turned real hot my first day on the roof was 91 degrees. The roof is sagging so it's hard to use a straight edge. I've tried the stair step method. It's taken me a week to do just half of the east roof.

9-27-1990 I fished Friday with the dinghy and 2 hp motor. It was real foggy and a good thing because fishing is closed on Fridays. A man rowed out and warned me. Lucille isn't talking to me because I reprimanded her for prevaricating. Mowed yard for the first time in quite a while

10-6-1990 Came up by myself. The Ranger now has 3,000 miles on it. Tasches dog "Mitzie" passed away while there were in the Dakotas on vacation.

11-5-1990 Mowed yard with Sears mower. Can't get a proper tide to change buoys. Lucille is back from Mexico she was gone for a week with the Putnams. What a waste of our lives. The commercial parasites are fishing up in our area now. We lit the oil stove this time as it got down to 39 degrees. J. Tasche is having some more remodeling done to his new house. We've had strangers around here for 7 years now, working on that place.

11-20-1990 Drained pipes. We had heavy flooding, especially at Skagit and Snohomish County. I'm now 67 years of age. We've had a 100 yr. flood over the Thanksgiving week!! Thousands of people are flooded out of their homes. Another catastrophe has been the sinking of the original I-90 floating bridge. I left my rain clothes on the north porch until Nov. 20th, nobody stole them. Chris is working in Sun Valley, Idaho at the ski resort.

12-6-1990 Bunny Mills our faithful dog passed away on 12-5-90 at 2:00 AM. Poor little girls' heart just gave out. We had a big storm after all the flooding and our beach has a whole bunch more logs. The storm came in conjunction with some 13 foot tides.

1-1-1991 We've had a helluva winter so far. We've had real icy snow storms and then some vicious wind storms. A lot of beach homes lost their bulkheads and foundations. Power was out to 100,000 homes twice. Trees smashed a zillion roofs and killed 2 separate people in their cars.

1-18-1991 We are at war with Iraq! Finally a sunny day today. Still have a log choked beach. Haven't changed out anchor yet.

17   JOURNAL # 4

This journal spans 19 years, from February of '91 to October of 2010 and is definitely the most poignant in terms of Wil's life. He will see the most changes and his outlook on life will change decidedly.

2-21-1991 Finally a sunny day after some heavy rain. All rivers came up to flood stage. We still cannot get out to the water because of all the logs.

3-13-1991 Brought up the Stihl 041 chain saw and chewed away on a couple logs. I came over on the ferry Kittitas. It has been remodeled to handle two levels of autos. The Iraq War is over!

3-20-1991 sunny today. Mowed with the Sears mower that we are trying to buy from Jeff. There were 2 eagles on the beach. Boeings is going to add 10,000 employees at Everett to build the 777. Chris is still working at Sun Valley, Idaho. I turned on the cold water for the first time this year.

4-11-1991 We had Lucille's relatives over for Easter in Kent. There were 14 of us. We've had the wettest spring April ever recorded. 5" already. A lot of houses have slid away. I cut some logs with the Stihl saw trying to make a path for our dinghy. I still have some huge ones to go. LeeRoy Young just completed his path through the logs to the water.

4-26-1991 LeeRoy Young's path to the water is closed again. Developers are trying to perc (a test used to determine septic viability) the lot across the street from us in Kent. The phone man left our phone turned over and broke Hazel's drop at her splice. His name is Bergman. I saw two grey whales swimming south today. The winter Brants have finally arrived. Chris is going to Alaska to be a commercial fisherman.

5-5-1991 Lucille finally came up to Whidbey to help out. We turned on the hot water. Bathroom sink supply line leaked, bought some cone washers at Jim's Hardware. We had a rabbit in our yard early in the morning and an otter had dinner on LeeRoy's buoy. The Starlings are trying to invade our cabin again! I put up a plywood barrier. Three grey whales have died in lower Puget Sound for some unknown reason. Chris is fishing for Sole in Dutch Harbor, Alaska.

5-14-1991 Lucille celebrated her 68th birthday up here digging some nice clams on a -3.5 tide. The rabbit is making a home in our yard. The road is still wet behind Diane's house. The otters are still here. The rabbit that has a home in the front yard has a little baby.

6-14-1991 Lucille got swamped in the Olympian. The ferry went by while we were getting ready to work on the buoy! That bastard ferry captain came in fast and left a huge wake.

The Olympian as it was found in 2012

7-13-1991 The water man and a contractor with backhoe and a dump truck finally fixed the water leak in the road behind Diane's. Diane's tap into the main was cracked. They raised her meter. It took about 6 hours of hard work. The idiots behind us shot a bunch of fireworks down on our roofs. The weather was tinder dry and

windy on the 4th of July. LeeRoy Young wasn't home. He would
have told 'em I'm pretty sure. We came up to guard our clams on a
-3.6 tide. Sure enough, Tasche's in-laws and their Spokane friends
dug on our beach. They hogged the beach and the water
department had us blocked in with their trucks so I scraped paint.

7-28-1991 I hauled away the Frigidaire refrigerator to Island
Recycle at Freeland. I took the doors off and trays out to lighten it.
It weighed 246 lb to start with. I used our little $7.00 dolly and our
boat dolly to get it out of our garage. LeeRoy helped me lift it into
the truck. I had to pay $5.00 at the recycle place. My automatic
transmission sprayed the truck, they seemed to have filled it too
full in Kent.

8-15-1991 Chris is down from his commercial fishing venture in
Alaska. Sandy is trying to sell her Mason Lake home for $150,000
to get out of debt. Evidently the French's have sold their Issaquah
home and have moved to a temporary location. Lucille never tells
me anything anymore. I painted a couple walls on the west side of
the house using Olympic overcoat paint. Jim Tasche is removing
paint from his house. He used Aspen paint without priming first
and the paint didn't stand up. The air show was spectacular at Paine
Field this year. They showed a "B-1B" Stealth Bomber and some
planes that had been in the Gulf War. Evidently Lucille is helping
Maridel move or something. She's down in Kent collecting mail
and watering the garden.

8-29-1991 We're having a wet Labor Day weekend. Kids above us
at the dentists' were throwing debris down on Tasche's place. I
yelled for them to cease and desist. They didn't so I went up and
told the homeowner in no uncertain terms that we don't tolerate
such nonsense. He apologized. I caught a few shakers and lost my
favorite strip rig in rough weather. I don't know whether my prop
cut it or what. Lucille hasn't talked to me for 5 days after she
botched a charity bag pick up in Kent.

9-7-1991 Lucille is still sulking and semi-silent as she has been
since August 27 (12 days). It really makes for a great life. She's
pleasant to everybody but me. I guess Chris has another car now
that he is back from fishing in Alaska. Lucille didn't actually tell

me.

9-10-1991 Came up alone and painted cabin skirting with Olympic oil stain "Cape Cod Grey". It looks like the J. Tasche's are repainting using my color! Gene Tasche's widow (Mrs. T) is also using my color! The commercial fishermen are really out in force. They are south of Possession. Simmon's garage is going to quit selling gas and oil! To update their tanks would be too costly! This is really bad news for us! I bought 5 gallons of stove oil from the Shell dealer and I think he is going to quit also! He charged me $1.50 per gallon!

9-23-1991 Came up alone again. Lucille is getting ready for a trip to Australia. I thought she's quit traveling after our little dog died. The commercial boys are fishing in area 8-2 now day and night. I painted some more cabin skirting with Olympic oil stain. Trolled in the afternoon at Clinton with the 2 H.P. Johnson, caught Shakers in 80 degree heat. We've been having a harvest moon, it rises at about 8 p.m. over north Everett. I painted the west drip caps with Olympic overcoat.

10-5-1991 Mowed with Sears mower. We haven't had any rain for 34 days! Lucille and M.D. are in Australia. I'm still picking tomatoes and cucumbers in Kent! Lindfors has hauled his boat out. LeeRoy is finally putting Washington numbers on his yellow boat instead of Oregon numbers.

10-14-1991 Lucille came back from Australia on 10-10-91. We have had a record 48 rainless days! The mountains look pretty bare. I started the 25 h.p/ Evinrude, washed and pumped the Skagit, and put the tarp back on.

10-27-1991 Came up alone. Lucille is too busy with her old maid friends and helping the French's move again to help me. I changed out the anchor block on a 7.2 low. Can't do it by myself on a much higher tide. We've finally had a couple days of rain and now things are getting cool (30 degrees). Mr. Young got a new wood stove.

11-2-1991 Drained pipes. We ate out on our 45 wedding anniversary at "Hung" Chinese restaurant.

12-2-1991 Came up after Thanksgiving Day windstorm. We are taking care of "Boswell" the French's dog while they are in Mexico for 10 days. Chris got a job directing cars at a shopping center parking lot.

12-19-1991 Lucille hasn't talked to me for a week. She thinks more of her old maid friends and miserable relatives than of me. I guess I've outlived my usefulness and she'll be glad when I'm out of the way. Ken's house in Kent is up for sale again, this time by some Florida jerks.

There he goes again - having a pity party! I wish he could see what is coming. Maybe he would appreciate what he has if he knew. Well I guess that is what this life and our lessons are all about. I've got some regrets, I suppose we all do, but some more than others. There's some things I would do differently if I could do it over again. Spend more time with my family is one thing I would do. My twin boys were working on the ferry by the time they were twelve years old. We all worked hard, it was a hard life. I don't know if I took the time to tell them how much I appreciated them. You know what they say? Hindsight is 20-20. Yessirree.

12-31-91 Our temporary buoy is gone. LeeRoy said Lindy saw it drift north then south way out. Bob Leaf has passed away. He died while in Barbados on a trip. Vern, Bob's brother-in-law is also dead. The widows must now take care of the Leaf place.

1-21-92 Stayed overnight to catch a high tide so I could float some logs to clear a path for the dinghy. It's easier to shift the logs with the water doing the work. J. Tasche's must be on a trip, they have taped their mailbox.

2-13-92 California has had their heaviest rain of the century after a long drought. 5 people have died. Our logs all came back, the path I had cleared is covered with more logs than ever. Chris failed miserably on shingling the new French's siding. He's found some other line of work, I don't know what happened to his new tool belt.

2-20-92 Having a lot of rain. Our Kent neighbors had another fight. The wife fired a pistol in the air to make her husband shape up after he flirted with a lady at the tavern. Jerry's wife was arrested.

2-28-92 J. Tasche has a new Chev 4x4 pickup with canopy and crew cab. Lindofrs has a 1985 Ford F150 4x4 with canopy. We have had a very mild winter. The farmers are picking their Daffodils already! They are worried about not having enough for the Easter floats.

3-8-92 Started to clear a path in the beach logs. Lucille is helping French's prepare to move to their new home. The nation has just had the mildest winter on record! 5 gallons of stove oil, $8.10!

3-2-92 No hot water yet. We are having a warm dry spring. California and Arizona are getting all the rain for a change. I mowed with the Firestone. Bob Leafs daughter Melody has had all the big fir trees on their property removed. I still haven't finished clearing a path for the dinghy. There was a big police search in Kent around 1:00 a.m. on 3-21-92. All the noise and spotlights and helicopters woke Lucille. Guess they were looking for car thieves. That Bell-Anderson Realtor is attracting these kooks with all his signs advertising the vacant lots on our street!

4-22-92 The state is spraying with helicopters down in southern King and Pierce counties. They think the Gypsy moth has been brought in from the far east on ships. We spent Easter at the Faber's this year. There were 11 of us. Chris had to work at Ocean Shores. Grace was recovering from a hip operation. Little Bud brought his girlfriend Megan. Big Bud's mother who is 92 came also. The double-decker ferry is back on our run. The World Fair happened 30 years ago.

5-17-92 Lucille is finally through helping the French's move around and found time to come up to Whidbey for the first time this year! The French's took us to dinner at the Sunset Café for Lucille's birthday and Mothers Day. It was a nice dinner, we all had Halibut cheeks. At Whidbey we mowed and moved logs. Our water meter still seems to be leading.

6-1-92 Came up alone. Lucille's friend Val's husband Dick passed away Saturday. He had a heart attack. Our weather for May was the driest on record. Several cities have water restriction and no lawn watering.

6-17-92 We sold our little Courier TF1640 to LeeRoy Young's son, Ron for $1,000. It had 56,500 miles on it. Lucille is going on another trip to Mexico, this time with Sandee and Grace. They leave tomorrow. Frances is quite ill after falling at her home. Mike the new water man is repairing quite a few leads along Columbia Beach Drive. It seems the plastic fittings break where the plastic pipe connects to the meter.

7-1-92 Gave some 1977 Ford shop manuals to the Young's for bird dogging the sale of our Courier to Ron Young. Lucille, Sandra and Grace just returned from Mexico last night after a couple weeks down there. While they were gone we broke a week of heat records here! We finally got an inch of rain on June 28th Yucca Valley, Calif. Had a huge earthquake (7.4) on that day. One child killed and 150 people hurt.

7-14-92 Lucille came up for the second time this year! We're finally getting an occasional day of rain. Water restrictions are still on thought. Seattle wants Everett water.

7-22-92 Lucille silent again for 4 days so far. No wonder my voice doesn't work. Brought up the 25 H.P. Evinrude. I think I'll get a new rinse barrel before I start it.

8-11-92 The lady at the new house south of the rental cabin fell while trying to launch her dinghy. She broke her leg. We're supposed to get some 90 degree weather for the next few days.

8-13-92 We finally launched the Skagit. We towed it with the Ranger. Lucille piloted the Skagit because she forgot her driver's license so she had to pilot instead of bringing back the truck and trailer. At the launch ramp an old fisherman gave us his leftover Herring. Lucille brought the Skagit to Columbia Beach slowly to conserve gas as we only had less than ½ tank. We still were able to troll for 3 hrs. and have a gallon left over.

9-21-92 Hauling down 25 H.P. Evinrude. She ran great this year. Tacked on a few shingles on garage and Lucille's bedroom. The Young's are on the Oregon coast. Two big hurricanes this fall - Andrew in Florida and Iniki in Hawaii.

10-11-92 I have been on jury duty the past week. I have one more week to go. Lucille has been no help. She and Barbara have gone to Hawaii. Mowed with Sears.

11-3-92 Came up alone on this election day. Lucille has sold our wonderful '84 Crown Victoria! She now has a little '92 "Probe" auto. It has about 100 miles on it as of today.

11-15-92 Up alone. Drained hot water tank. Puttied some windows. Worked on Skagit steering cable. Tasche's are still gone. Hazel's son-in-law passed away in Florida. We had 2 kids at Kent for Halloween.

12-2-92 Checked pipes, drained gate valve. Came up alone.

12-12-92 We have new neighbors across the street in Kent. Lucille left her Probe hatchback open and the battery went dead. The U.S. Marines are in Somalia feeding starving blacks.

1-30-93 Nice Sunny day. We had a vicious windstorm on Jan 20. It did millions of damage. Jim clocked it at 60 m.p.h. A tree fell on Mrs. Engstrom's in Kent. LeeRoy Young is in the Coupeville hospital with a blood clot in his leg. His dad just had a perforated ulcer operation. The wind blew some shingles off Jim's house and our garage and porch and bent our TV antenna element. We had water in the toilet tank again so I turned the tank faucet off. Our tulips are coming up.

2-13-93 The little house north of Addy's has been moved out. Probably another yuppie mansion going to replace it. LeeRoy's dad died today at 4:00 a.m. LeeRoy is hobbling around after 10 days in the hospital with a blood clot in his leg. J. Tasche left today for Mexico. He took his trailer and is traveling with a group of trailer people. I tacked on some ridge shingles lost in the Jan 20th storm. The roof is slippery.

2-27-93 Lucille has gone to work for the French's today instead of helping me. Burroughs and his neighbor are going to put in concrete bulkheads this spring.

3-11-93 The weather is perfect today. Lucille flew to Turkey today! Ron is helping LeeRoy on his unpaid day off. He brought our old Courier up. It's running great after a carburetor rebuild. Ron has the canopy off.

3-27-93 Lucille got back from Turkey on 3-22-93. She didn't even mention that I fixed the doorbell and painted the utility room semi-gloss white Dutch Boy. She's so busy with her relatives and old maid friends she doesn't pay any attention to me.

4-14-93 I turned on the cold water. Maridel cut her finger on Easter Day. Mowed with Sears.

5-13-93 I bought a fish & chip takeout dinner from the new restaurant at the ferry landing. The price was $5.69 for the large order. The dinner was quite good. 4 lg. pieces of fish, lots of fries and good tartar sauce.

6-3-93 Mowed with Firestone. Lucille came up for the first time this year! We turned on the hot water. I dove with skin suit and finally found our anchor chair on the second day. Lucille dug 3 clams. I took them down to change the water and the seagulls stole them.

6-30-93 We bought our fishing licenses for a total cost of $8.00. Lucille's license was free as she is now a 70 yr. old woman. The old Taylor house is for sale. 2 bdrms and bath and a half for $349,000. Mowed with Firestone. LeeRoy gave us a nice crab.

7-25-93 Came up alone. Lucille went to a play with M.D. Sandee and Grace. I removed tarp from Skagit and hooked up the 18 H.P. Evinrude.

8-2-93 Fished for the first time this year. We have had a grey, wet summer til Seafair Week. The Winston hydro did a spectacular flip. French's have a new dog named Bunter Gilmore. His job is to chase the deer away.

8-8-93 I finally caught a big King in the Olympian dinghy and 2 h.p. Johnson. I caught him at about 8:15 a.m. using chrome brass dodger and Lucille's new Herring aid by Les Davis. I hooked him just north of Jim & Johns. He weighed about 20 pounds. It took about ½ hour to land. The Herring I used was one we had left over from 1992. The wind was from the south,, the tide was incoming.

8-17-93 We shopped on the way up at Woodinville. Lucille went back to Kent after a couple days. I've stayed up to shingle the southeast hip portion of the cabin. Looks like it will take 2 bundles. The job is time consuming because the hip angle shingles have to be cut for each row and flashing has to be woven in on the north side. As soon as I stripped the old shingles the annual migration of little flies arrived and started harassing me. They just appear for a day and die.

8-26-93 Lindy is catching more Kings at Humpie Hollow. They have poured Burroughs bulkhead. He installed a memorial plaque to honor his parents, their ashes were dropped in the Sound out front. The contractor is working on Bill's at the same time. He lost a home to a slide down by Possession in the thirties.

9-16-93 Widow Tasche's son-in-law helped me push logs, seems like a nice man. I trolled with the 2 h.p. Johnson, just shakers and a couple bumps. Lucille has gone to Hawaii with Chris. Not a very nice thing to do right in the middle of my precious short fishing season. She gave me 2 days notice. She's going to be gone from 9-14 to 9-24-93. My F-100 truck passed the emission test. The test cost $12.00. It's a new deal for small cities and King county.

9-26-93 Lucille and Chris are back from Hawaii. That trip ruined my precious fishing time. That was very inconsiderate of Lucille and Maridel. I'm up here by myself because Lucille has jet lag. I puttied some windows and scraped paint on the bathroom west wall.

Wil is still quite bitter and angry with Lucille. He expects her to be here to help him fish and blames her for ruining his fishing. She is gone a lot now and doesn't come up to the cottage much at all anymore. I don't enjoy watching them much anymore as they sure

*don't seem happy like they were a few decades ago. They are 70
years old now, not much time left to enjoy one another.*

9-27-93 The house on the north side of Addie's house is being
framed up. I guess it is also going to be a 3 story house! They are
going to have an elevator! The weather has been superb this
September with only a trace of rain! Still don't see any commercial
fishermen up in our area.

9-28-93 I finally got up to the Chinese restaurant Hong Kong
Gardens for a take-out dinner. I had No. 3. Soup, egg roll, almond
fried chicken, beef Chow Uk, pork fried rice, tea, fortune cookie.
$7.50. Looks like it will make 2 meals. Red Fox caught an 8 lb.
Blackmouth today at Glendale.

10-10-93 Came up alone. Painted the utility room ceiling green
latex. I golfed at the par 3 golf course on the French Road. It's a
beautiful course, lots of trees. It costs $5.00 for nine. You pay on
the honor system, put your money in an old milk can. I started the
18 h.p. We didn't even launch the Skagit this year. Lucille took a
trip right in the heart of fishing season. Can't remember such a dry
fall with so many flat calm days. Columbia Beach is getting to be a
tall house beach. Every yuppie tries to block his neighbors view
and sunshine. Sports fishing is closed in area 8-2.

11-30-93 Part of the garage shingles blew off. I patched the spot
temporarily. Lucille and French's have gone to Guatemala. Lucille
gave me 6 hours notice! She just got through ruining my fishing
season by going to Hawaii with Chris and now this, nobody cares
anymore.

12-12-93 We've had heavy rains this month and winds. The logs
have stacked up out front again. There are too many full time
yuppies on the beach now. They push the logs to us. Lucille
returned from Guatemala on Dec. 6th. I shaved off my mustache on
Nov. 21, she didn't even notice till Dec. 11th!

1-16-94 Lucille and Maridel have gone to Sandee's Shelton home
for the weekend. I had to come up alone. Mild winter so far. Mr.
Young has a big roof drainage project going. He has a big load of

gravel in the yard. Melody is living in their new mansion two houses south of my little cabin.

1-28-94 Started oil stove. I turned on the water as I am staying overnight to push logs. The logs have blocked our dinghy path but none are too huge. Val's son passed away on 1-26 in San Francisco. He was 35 years old. Lucille and I went to Chet and Ruth's 50th wedding anniversary celebration. Lucille bought some new chair pads for the Kent kitchen so I brought the old ones to Whidbey. L.A. had a 6.6 earthquake on Jan. 17th.

2-20-94 Came up alone. Some new logs on our beach. Some more shingles blew off our garage. The shingles aren't too bad but the nails have rusted away!

3-26-94 Mowed with Sears mower. Pushed logs. Used space heaters. Temperatures at night in the low thirties. Beautiful full moon and clear 60 degree days. Melody and her boy also pushed logs. The ferry Cathlamet lost control and hit the Mukilteo dock. The Chelan is subbing in.

5-3-94 Things are really going to pot. Fishing for Salmon has been closed this year in our zone 8-2 and 8-1 from May 1 thru October! I golfed the front nine at the restored Holmes Harbor golf course! It has been restored by Jack Sikma Enterprises to wonderful condition. Lucille has gone on another short notice trip! She is in Mexico. She left April 30. I had the mail stopped. I cut some beach logs with the Stihl saw and put some beach gravel under the south stepping stones.

5-24-94 Lucille came up for the first time this year!! We put out the buoy, the tide was -3.3. I used my skin suit with new gloves and hat. Lucille dug 40 clams out of one hole while I was fooling with the anchor! We golfed at the Island Greens (French Road) golf course. Pushed logs.

6-21-94 Came up Tuesday evening. Mowed with Firestone. My weed-eater handle broke in half. Lucille dug 40 more huge clams for Maridel! The neighbors large orange buoy went adrift at about 9:00 p.m.. Lucille and I launched our dinghy to retrieve it as most of the neighbors weren't home. Melanie and Galen are being harassed by the grumpy old men, LeeRoy and Lindy for leaving their log fire burning and smoldering for days on end.

7-31-94 I just finished 4 days jury duty in superior court. We found Leonard B. guilty of drug selling. That's my third jury duty! The swallows are still in our attic and have 2 babies. We blocked the swallows from entering our attic. The super carrier Abraham Lincoln is coming to Everett on 8-3-94. The Island County Port is working on the Mosquito Fleet dock. It's going to be located adjacent to the Clinton Ferry dock on the north side.

8-14-94 I scrubbed out buoy. King fishing has opened in Elliot Bay after the Indians started to gillnet. The sports fishermen had to surround the gillnetters in order to get the fisheries attention! I pushed another big log off our beach on an 11.5 tide.

9-6-94 We've been dog sitting Bosley Jr. over the long Labor Day weekend. Sure ties a person down. I finally came up today and mowed with Firestone. Lots of boats out today. 2 Navy ships are berthed at the new Everett Navy Base. The Indians have taken a test netting, if they catch enough they might let sports fishermen have a few scraps.

10-9-94 We are just using our electric heaters as our oil stove is not getting fuel in the carburetor. Lucille likes her new Rival heater.

11-28-94 Lucille is in Texas with Sandee, Grace and Maridel. I put 8x10 tarps on the Skagit and Olympian. They cost $4.96 each from Ernst Hardware in Kent. Lucille bought her own Christmas presents. One was a treadmill walking machine.

12-11-94 A couple tie down ropes were untied on our 8x10 tarp on the Skagit. It's an enigma as to how that happened. Maybe the wind did it. Lucille is back from Texas.

12-28-94 We've had record rains this month. 17" of rain for the month at Port Orchard. Our dinghy path has closed again. Chris is going to college at Central in Ellensburg, Washington. Lucille got an answering machine for Christmas and I got a cordless phone.

1-21-95 Pruned tree. 181818 on Ranger odometer. Lucille had gallbladder removed at Swedish Hospital.

2-4-95 Lucille still recovering from her gallbladder operation. I was sick 3 days last week. Lots of logs out front. J. Tasche mowed our yard because I was ill!

4-6-95 Mowed with Sears. Have been ill with Shingles. Am under doctors care. Lucille drove and weeded.

4-21-95 Had last visit to doctor for my Shingles. I'm still not completely recovered. I mowed with Sears rotary today. The gray whales have been showing in front of our place. Lucille weeded and I drove the Ranger.

5-4-95 Lucille left for Europe today with Bonnie and the French's. She didn't even wait til I recovered fully from the Shingles. That was pretty cruel on her and Maridel's part, but what goes around comes around. My eye is still a little bloodshot and my breathing is wheezy. I mowed and repaired the picnic table leg.

5-14-95 Lucille is still away on a trip. I mowed and took a load of limbs to the Langley sewage plant. My eye is still bloodshot and I'm wheezing. Gert Tasche was following a truck hauling a shed. The shed fell off and crashed into Gert's car, ruining the Buick. They are back in the Dakotas buying a new one.

5-30-95 Moved some logs with the "come along" tool. We have had 2 weeks of terrific weather, every day over 75 degrees! Lucille came back from Europe. Fishing is not going to open until Aug 1 and close Sept 30th! A lot of marine stores are closing. We had our 1st hamburgers and shakes from the new Dairy Queen in Clinton.

6-14-95 Mowed with Firestone. Mr. Young is ill with the flu. Lucille and I moved some more logs using the "come along" blocks. The J. Tasche's are back from the Dakotas. They replaced their damaged Buick Le Sabre with another one that is 3 years newer. We put out a temporary buoy. We used the Norfloat red buoy that drifted by our cabin on 6-23-94. We put 15' of polypropylene line on it at .15 cents per foot. Lucille did a lot of the work out of the Olympian dinghy. Lucille dug clams getting some huge ones. Our water pipes are chattering so bad at night that I had to go out in the middle of the night and turn the water off. We can't figure it out!

6-22-95 Lucille put new bedspreads on the guest bedroom bed. They are from Mervyns Dept. store. I haven't had a haircut in 6 months recovering from the Shingles. Fishing is closed in our area. Our water pipes still chatter late at night.

7-13-95 We brought Marian's dog Bosley up here for the first time. He is one year old. We are dog sitting because Bob French's father passed away and they had to fly to Los Angeles for his funeral. He died of cancer. Gert Tasche's brother is visiting again, he vacations here just about every year. A boat with three people on board collided with the ferry Cathlamet. A ferry worker had to leap in and help rescue them, the accident happened on July 12th.

8-13-95 Bought fishing license at Sebo's. Cost was $14.00. This year fishing is just open from Aug 1st thru Sept 30. Lucille doesn't care to fish anymore, she did not buy a license!

8-31-94 Came up alone! Lucille had to have a check up so she can go on a trip to Branson, Mo. She is going right in the middle of my precious fishing month. I trolled with the Olympian dinghy and the 2 h.p. Johnson. Used Lucille's pole because it had a white dodger and put on a pink and white squid. A big fish bit and I didn't give enough slack, so the fish broke the line and I lost dodger, sinker and squid.

9-10-95 Lucille has gone on another trip, right in the heart of fishing season. She has gone by auto to Missouri. I replaced Lucille's dodger and squid with new ones from Birdies of Kent. The new pink squid is a single hook mini squid by Challenger from Zak Tackle Mfg. It gets a lot of strikes.

9-20-95 Lucille is still on a trip to Branson, Mo. The weather here is still great. Carol has some women friends visiting from Wisconsin. I guess they're out here looking for work.

9-29-95 Mowed with Sears mower in between rain storms. Lucille returned from her trip to Branson, MO. The Humpie run was the biggest in 32 years. Lucille's trip ruined my fishing season.

10-15-95 The state is going to remodel Clinton ferry dock making it larger. They eventually want ferries to come in every 20 minutes! Lucille has quit coming up for the year! I still can't get oil to the carburetor of the oil stove. The Sound is brown from all the flood waters there has been so much rain. Toilet closet filled even though water was off.

11-10-95 Temp in cabin 38 degrees. Planted 2 tulip bulbs from Fred Meyers. Carol is back from Alaska. LeeRoy gave me a nice telephone directory. Raked leaves. Crawled under house looking for oil leaks. Roof O.K. Lucille was quite ill 2 days ago, vomited quite a bit. She seems OK today. She went to French's to do accounting on the computer.

12-13-95 Terrible storm last night. 86 mpg winds at Mukilteo. 120 mph wind at Crystal Mountain. We lost a couple shingles on the garage. Our logs are all clogged up again. The ferries had to stop running during the storm. I've never seen so many logs adrift. The ferry just crept along avoiding the debris. I saw some blackfish amongst the logs.

12-23-95 Sea lion in front of our cabin. Tried to start oil stove. Couldn't keep oil flowing. I've had to resort to electric space heaters. The cabin temp. was 30 degrees at 11am. The dinghy path is closed again. This is getting to be a pain.

1-23-96 Our temporary buoy drifted away because Lucille wouldn't help me bring it in last fall. 34 degrees in the cabin.

2-12-96 Had to pull dinghy over all the logs. Lucille gave me no help. Nice calm sunny day after our horrendous floods.

2-26-96 Logs shifted all around, we are back to square one.

3-26-96 Mowed with Sears. Carol had a man mowing her yard. Shingles starting to blow off garage.

4-5-96 Cleared some more logs from the dinghy path. Lucille and Maridel have gone to Hong Kong. They left on the 2nd and will return on April 11th. I'm home alone for Easter. Robbie has a new car. He wrecked his pickup a few months ago.

4-20-96 Mowed with Sears mower. Our lilacs are blooming and we have 2 tulips. I still haven't turned on the hot water. The oil stove is not getting oil. Some shingles have blown off the south half of the garage roof. Lucille and Maridel are back from Hong Kong China.

5-5-96 Lucille came up for the first time this year. She dug some nice clams on a -2.1 tide. I used the Stihl saw on the dinghy path logs.

5-16-96 Came up alone. I worked about 6 more hours trying to clear a dinghy path. Lucille bought a new mattress for the Kent house. LeeRoy Young and spouse are taking a cruise to Alaska soon.

6-11-96 We have a little rabbit living in our garage. We brought up the 19" Magnavox TV to put on our Sauder Model 5155 TV VCR cart. We turned on the oil stove. After hearing some bubbling, the oil finally started to flow into the stove. Pulled another log out of the dinghy path with the "come along" tool. I sawed off a log under the house that was evidently used to skid the cabin onto the lot. Sonics finally won a game from the Chicago Bulls.

6-30-96 Sandee piled up her Nissan for the second time. A man hit her from behind. Her airbag deployed. She has a bruised chest. His car is totaled. I dove again on a -3.1 tide. The new hat and gloves are a great improvement. The water was nice and calm. Salmon fishing is closed in area 8-2. A huge run of Sockeye are going through the locks.

7-10-96 Vandals broke Jim's mailbox and got into Nelsons freezer at 4:00 pm on 7-11-96. We hauled mattress and springs to dump. I painted east side of cabin.

7-26-96 The weather has been very hot for a week, 90 degrees every day. Fishing is still closed in area 8-2. Lindy bought a new aluminum "Lund" boat and sold his smaller aluminum boat. J. Tasche sold his aluminum boat. More and more jet skis are showing up along our beach, they are very aggravating.

8-16-96 They have quietly opened fishing in area 8-2. No Kings can be kept. A record Sockeye run occurred this year in Lake Washington - 400,000 fish.

8-26-96 Brought up second gold rocking chair. Melody is trying to sell her house for $850,000. Melody has opened a skin care and make over shop in Langley. My stomach was really upset on some of Lucille's cooking. Lucille's shoulder is troubling her. Tasche's are heating with gas now.

9-18-96 The tax assessor stopped by. He wanted to know if we had rug and vinyl floor covering, type of wall covering (he put down sheetrock because it is cheaper). He also wanted to know if we had a wood stove and the type of foundation we had. He then admired our roof. Lucille has to dog sit Bosley right during our precious fishing season. So I'm here alone. The ferry Kitsap ran aground at Rich passage in the fog. President Clinton visited Seattle. The assessor said he would call our ceilings acoustical because it's cheaper than our wood ceilings.

10-2-96 I'm still trying to fix the oil stove. Can't get the oil to reach the stove. I came up alone again. Lucille had to go to Homemakers Club Reunion.

10-12-96 Carol our neighbor to the north has returned from Alaska. Tasches, our neighbor to the south are away. Lucille is going to Mexico with Ann. She gave me one day's notice! The average man would never tolerate what I have to go through. I'm thinking seriously about kicking her out when she gets back, then she and Maridel can use their giggling secrets on some other sucker. I don't feel like I'm part of this secretive family anymore. I just don't feel at ease, wondering what their next selfish trick is going to be.

10-26-96 Lucille came back from Mexico, Oct. 24th at 8pm. Worked on oil line, still a problem. We had a bad wind storm more shingles blew off garage. We are dog sitting again.

11-1-96 Putnams stayed overnight while we are still dog-sitting. Lucille didn't let me know ahead of time about any of it. Now Lucille is not talking, makes for a real jolly 50th anniversary which occurs in 3 hours. I'm staying overnight on Halloween, no kids came by.

11-9-96. Lucille didn't have any kids at Kent on Halloween either. Mowed with Sears mower. Got a nice Nokia cell phone for our 50th anniversary. I called Kent and it worked fine. We've only made 2 calls. I received one and I sent one for a minute and a half total. Oil still not getting to the oil stove unless pumped in.

11-23-96 I'm another year older. My good friend Royal passed away on 11-7-96. We have had a heavy snowstorm, 12" at Everett. I'm draining the hot water tank today. The temperature was only 25 degrees in the cabin when I arrived. Called home again on the cell phone !! Drained pipes. Closed hot faucet. Got a nice ANS computer and H.P. printer for my birthday.

12-7-96 Pearl Harbor Day. Rainy day, very heavy snowpack in the mountains already. Temp. 38 degrees in the cabin. Our power has been off again up here. Lucille had to go to French's to bake fruitcakes today. Bud won $900.00 at Reno a couple weeks ago, on my birthday. Chris has his own house in Kirkland now.

1-5-97 We had a mudslide that has just about wiped us out! Our garage is totaled. J. Tasche is draining water thru our yard after calling for permission. His place is O.K., ours is a shambles. Some of our foundation posts are tilting, our garage is full of mud.

Oh this was a bad slide for the little cottage, pretty much filled the yard with mud and the garage took the brunt of the slide. A tree did hit the corner of the cottage and moved it at least 6". Wil will spend years shoveling mud out of the garage, never to recover it. There was just too much mud for one man in his 70's to take care of. This plus his anger with Lucille contributes to his giving up on his happy adventure with his fishing cottage. After this it seems pretty much like all work and no fun.

1-11-97 Came up again to start restoring our property. I still don't trust the bud bank behind us so I won't stay overnight yet.

1-24-97 No change, still a muddy mess. Our cabin has shifted 6" east on the north end. Still risky to stay overnight.

2-2-97 Wheeled some more mud out of the yard. CAN Insurance rejected our damage claims, both at Kent for the oil tank and at Whidbey for the catastrophic slide.

2-8-97 Cabin still standing, but leaning a little on the north end. LeeRoy gave me a new phone book. We've just had a week of dry weather, so I'm up shoveling mud. We're communicating with our new cell phone quite a bit.

2-23-97 Still moving mud. Melody has taken her "for Sale" sign down because so many looky lou's were trespassing on her property. Our tulips survived the slide on west side of the house!

3-24-97 Ray passed away on 3-23-97. I'm still shoveling mud and debris out of garage.

4-1-97 Now we had a terrible 70 mph windstorm. It blew all of the shingles off the south side of our garage roof! I'm getting sick of this place, it's too hard on my health. A tree blew down on a man's truck on the Mukilteo Speedway and killed the man's wife on Easter. I still haven't had time to turn on the water or mow the lawn.

4-12-97 Shoveled garage mud. Put adjustable post under north center beam. LeeRoy cut down Diane's apple trees, now we can see Mt. Baker again.

4-18-97 Shoveled mud. Mowed with Sears mower. Bomb threat on the Bainbridge Island run today.

4-26-97 Mowed with Sears. I'm short of breath lately, takes me quite a while to finish. Turned on the cold water for the first time this year. Our Kent area code is changing tomorrow. I've been calling Kent with our cell phone. It has really been handy for keeping in touch. 70 degrees today.

5-8-97 Stayed overnight and the cabin didn't fall down. Mowed with Sears. Haven't turned on hot water yet. Am having trouble breathing and having to rest a lot when I mow. I think we're going to have to have the mowing done for us, I can't keep up much longer, am too old. Weather was so nice I am staying over one more night. Shoveled more mud out of garage. The Assessor has lowered our cabin value to $20,000 after being hit by the 100 year storm. Bought a Dairy Queen hamburger. Looks like Orientals own the D.Q.

5-18-97 Mowed with Sears. Lucille has gone to Mexico again! I'm having more trouble breathing. I get exhausted mowing the lawn, it takes me about 5 hours because of a lot of rests. Lucille is showing me no mercy. Haven't turned on the hot water yet. Everett's aircraft carrier cruised by at 9:10am. It is really huge.

6-5-97 Lucille came up to see the storm damage. She mowed the yard. I'm too exhausted to do much of it. We've had a terrible wet spring. Melody's new house is falling apart already. The lawn mowing is too much for us, we're trying to hire someone.

9-6-97 We finally came up to Whidbey again. I had to take a sabbatical leave to have a laryngectomy and tracheotomy. I can no longer speak. On July 11th my voice box was removed. I use an artificial larynx purchased from Spokane, cost $700.00! A local gardener has been mowing our yard. New people have purchased Melody's big house. They have 3 big dogs. Our picnic table leg has finally broken. The table must have been 25 years old. Our garage is still full of mud and the garage roof is stripped of its shingles. The cabin is still teetering on tilted foundation posts. Lucille bought our lunch at Dairy Queen. Replaced some garage shingles and put on temporary 30 lb roll roofing. Pruned blackberries growing in garage.

So now Wil can no longer talk without his voice-box. For a guy who was already lonely, that is quite a blow! I'm worried about

137

him, it seems he is in a string of bad luck. He surely is not very happy anymore.

9-13-97 Put on another row of Blue Label Red Cedar shingles that survived the New Year's Eve mud slide. Edge grain, clear heart wood. I put these on our leaning garage. I'm on my 18th radiation session. The new people's dogs are pooping in our yard.

9-20-97 Shingled garage roof. Am still having radiation treatments on my throat. I'm up to 22 treatments. Mr. Young has a new cyclone fence on south side of his property.

9-28-97 Singled more garage roof. I have one more week of radiation on my throat. Our roofing paper blew partially off the garage again.

10-15-97 Took a load of lawn waste to Langley sewage plant. I have graduated from the Virginia Mason radiation lab. After 33 sessions of 5 megavolts. My skin ended up pretty toasted. My throat was sore. My last day was Oct. 6. Carol is just back from Alaska today. The temperature is 71 today.

11-1-97 Our anniversary. I came up alone and shoveled more dirt out of garage. Today is nice, 60 degrees, calm and sunny. Kevin is still mowing our yard.

11-9-97 Beautiful day, shoveled more dirt out of garage. Maridel is away on another damn trip. Didn't even stay home for her anniversary. She's in Mexico.

11-23-97 Made it to my birthday! Shoveled more mud out of shed. Came up in the rain. Very rough on the Sound! I called Lucille at Marian's in Issaquah on our cell phone. I also speed dialed our Kent phone on our cell phone. Lucille pulled a sly one on me. She said she was going to visit Sandee at Shelton, instead they went to McMinnville, Oregon, I had no idea where they were! Nice family. That happened on 11-20-97.

12-3-97 Shoveled more mud, trimmed fir tree. 36 degrees in cabin. El Nino weather. Someone has been fooling with our water meter.

1-10-98 Made it to 1998. It's just 25 degrees inside and outside the cabin. Somebody left some bags of trash in our yard, it's always something. We're supposed to get snow tonight!

2-1-98 Made it to February. Shoveled more garage mud. We've had a couple record warm days for January. The French's bought a new Subaru auto. I'm still eating "Ensure" products.

2-22-98 Lucille passed away at 1:00 pm on Feb. 19th, 1998. She had a heart attack in bed at our Kent home at 12:30am on the 18th. Carol and the Youngs were very sympathetic.

That's it, just the facts. I know he has to be feeling something. His wife just died. Even though they weren't talking much anymore, he had loved her for so many years. They had been together 52 years. He doesn't have many friends at this point in his life. Oh he is going to be so alone. My heart aches for him. This is what I saw coming for him when he was saying to himself such things as 'she will miss me when I'm gone' - he didn't think she would be the one going.

3-14-98 Kevin is mowing our yard again this year. He does a real good job. I visited the radiologist on 3-11 at Valley Medical Center. Lucille has a nice grave at the Tahoma National Cemetery, Section 15, plot 98. People left a lot of flowers at the grave. I shoveled more mud out of shed.

3-29-98 Beautiful clear day today. Gert was really sorry to hear of Lucille's death while they were away. South Whidbey Record published a great obituary. Mr. & Mrs. Young saved the paper for me. Lots more flowers have been placed on Lucille's grave. I shoveled more dirt today.

4-16-98 We had a nice memorial for Lucille at the French mansion. About 50 people attended. Dorothy was there tethered to her oxygen tank. 90 year old Agnes was there with her walker. I'm shoveling more dirt out of the garage. The rabbits are nesting in our front yard again.

5-11-98 Shoveled dirt. I haven't had a phone call from a family member for one full month. Now I know how my mother felt when she was widowed.

5-30-98 More shoveling. They have had 3" of rain since 5-11. Still have rabbits. I was the only one to put flowers on Lucille's grave for Memorial Day.

6-11-98 More shoveling in garage. Still haven't turned on water. They had an avalanche on Mt. Rainier today. The Evans called me to see how I was doing. The only call I've had from Lucille's side of the so-called family was a message from Chris on the answering machine telling me he had used some of my Vacation Internationale points. The state is going to work on the Mukilteo Ferry dock this weekend, so the ferry must go to Edmonds.

6-22-98 Got a nice Father's Day card from the French's. The weeds were just about to go to seed in the front yard. Took the yard waste to Langley.

7-9-98 Shoveled garage dirt. Patched north porch roof, pulled beach weeds. Stayed overnight, still haven't turned on hot water. Pipe leaks from tank to toilet. Lindy has been out fishing and crabbing in his Lund boat. Still no calls from Lucille's side of the family.

7-19-98 Took garbage to Bayview, $5.96 for 1st can and $2.00 something for an additional can. Patched roof. No calls.

7-26-98 I'm working on the toilet. I shifted the tank ¾" to the east so the spud will fit better. I haven't reattached it to the wall yet, so the tank is resting on some automobile jack stands. Still no phone calls.

8-5-98 Put 2 new stainless 2 and ½" #14 round head Philips screws in the toilet tank. I used my Sears right angle drill accessory to drill inside the tank, it was a life saver. I've had it for several years, that's about the first time I've used it. It's been 85-90 degrees every day for a week. I saw the new navy ship heading south from Everett to Seattle. The ship is for beach landings. It carries several huge hover craft. The hover craft can go up to 80 mph. Got a 2 minute call from Chris telling me he was going to use some more of my time share points. He accused me of not paying the annual dues ($1,000) on time. He arranged to have a dunning letter sent to me. He says the reason he has to use the time share points is because I'm not using them. I asked him if he knew Lucille and I had a 50th wedding anniversary. No he hadn't heard about that. I guess that's why we didn't get a card.

8-15-98 We had our first rain in about 3 weeks today. Lucille and my headstone is finally installed at the cemetery. Trimmed fir tree. Had deluxe hamburger, Blizzard, and small fries at Dairy Queen. $4.39. Sanded bathroom door with No. 60 sandpaper on a sanding block.

8-26-98 Still no rain. I sawed part of the log under the house that was used to move the cabin up the beach. It has started to pull away from the floor joists, kind of dangerous to crawl under it. I pruned the fir tree. LeeRoy Young has offered to haul the limbs away because they were blocking his million dollar view. So that saved me some trips to Langley.

9-12-98 Pruned Fir tree again. Mr. Young took the other limbs away. Sawed some more under the cabin on the old logs used to skid the cabin up the beach. We've had one month without rain. On my last appointment with the doctor, he made me have a chest X-ray. He called to say he wants me to have a cat scan. He says it's nothing to worry about. I didn't call back for a week so they called me again. So I've got to call and have them help me make an appointment.

9-20-98 Had a chest CT scan at Valley Radiologists. Dr. H. of Virginia Mason recommended it. I trimmed the Fir tree some more. Quite foggy til noon on 9-21-98.

9-28-98 Hauled Fir limbs to sewage plant. My chest scan turned out OK. I was going to paint fascia board but my paint had dried up. That was good paint. I sawed another length of the skid log under the cabin.

10-25-98 Trimmed the Fir tree. French's are on a trip from Oct 24

- Nov 4. Chris will take care of the dogs and me.

11-9-98 Trimmed Fir tree.

12-3-98 Windstorm blew felt paper off garage and blew aluminum ridge off west bedroom. I had to carefully crawl up and repair them. November had record rain.

12-17-98 The weather is supposed to become very cold this weekend so I'm draining the pipes. President Clinton has started to bomb Baghdad again. He is diverting attention away from his possible impeachment.

1-2-99 Up for first time in 1999. We have had temperatures in the teens for several days in a row. It appears the pipes and toilet survived although I haven't turned anything on.

2-14-1999 Valentines' Day, my first one alone after 52 years. We've had a very wet winter. A slide hit a house at Brighton Beach. We looked at some property there before we bought this place. Windstorm blew a shingle off the main roof, west peak.

3-6-99 This is the first sunny day we've had in 88 days! Mt. Baker has had 900" of snow since Oct. 98. 29 degrees this morning.

3-20-99 I found a blown 20 amp fuse this time. The refrigerator was off and the living room outlets also. The water in the ice trays had melted. I talked to LeeRoy Young for a couple minutes, that's one of the rare times anybody has talked to me, most of my life is in complete silence now.

That is perhaps the saddest thing I have ever heard someone say. He has been a long time building up to this place in his life. One-by-one any connections Wil had in life have dropped away. He had a hand in many of them, and it looked more like pushing them away than their dropping away. Living a life in silence sure magnifies the loneliness. I wonder if Wil believes he has a purpose and reasons to live for? I'd like to prod him as he sits there in the cottage, all alone. I'd like to tell him, but I can't. So I look on and it makes me sad too. It reminds me of the lonely times I spent in my life. They were wasted times. It was so much more fun to watch him and Lucille get all excited about fishing. This isn't fun.

4-11-99 The gray whales were in front of the Clinton ferry dock today. French's offered to take me to the Easter dinner this year but I went to the cemetery instead. The Lovell's brought me a fancy ham dinner. The Young's are pulling logs off the beach today.

4-25-99 I used the new farm jack to move some logs off the ramp. It seems to work quite well. I turned on the cold water for the first time this year.

5-9-99 Mother's Day without mother. The weather has been very cold and wet so far this year. Mt. Baker broke the world snow record held by Mt. Rainier since 1970. Mt. Baker had 90' of snow. The D.O.T. is just now opening North Cascades and Chinook passes. I won $500.00 on Keno about the time I had to pay $500.00 for my Ranger tune up.

6-6-99 Rained today. Found a dead seal on our beach. A lot of Grey whales have been dying in Puget Sound this year. The Makah Indians harpooned a whale this spring.

6-12-99 My old toilet broke. It's been cracked for a long time. I was planning on staying a few days, but can't now.

6-17-99 Disconnected the old toilet and tank. I think the code only allows the small 1.6 gal tanks now. I think I'm going to have to call a plumber to cut off the soil pipe and install the toilet. In the mean time, I'm all shut down.

6-27-99 I cut off the soil pipe with a hacksaw. It took me about 4 hours. Very cool and wet spring and summer this year. Skiers are still skiing. Today is the last day for the mariners in the Kingdome. 32,668,000 attended the Kingdome during its lifetime.

7-8-99 Still no toilet. I fooled around trying to put another board around the toilet waste pipe so the flange screws would hold better. Nothing went right so I'm still working on it. I called around for toilets. They have to order them. The toilets arrive on the Tuesday and Friday shipment. It's a good thing I came up, I had left some bananas and the trash bag since 6-27-99.

7-18-99 I bought an Eljer Patriot toilet at East Hill Hardware. It cost $83.00. I was trying to get the old toilet supply faucet off and I broke the end of the nipple that comes through the wall. I had to take out the flour bin to see how bad the damage was behind the wall. I also made about 4 trips to the hardware to get some new pipes. The weather was 80 degrees but I didn't get to see much of it. I haven't turned the water on yet. I didn't finish the toilet yet. I wanted to get rid of that faucet for 40 years.

8-4-99 A large rabbit befriended me. He came right up to me and let me pet him. We've had severe lightning storms for the past 4 days with over 3,000 strikes. A lot of animals have run away, maybe that's where he came from. He's not a cottontail. He's much larger.

8-18-99 I painted the bare spot in the bathroom with Glidden Interior Spred Latex with Teflon for kitchen bath & trim. Purchased from Fred Mayer. The color is called "Cozy Light". The clerk had to mix in his computerized machine. The large rabbit is still here. I was trimming the grass at the edge of the garage and he tried to help out.

9-2-99 The large rabbit still comes to greet me. They are still working on the roof of the house above mine. They are also still working on the Clinton Ferry dock.

10-17-99 Nice sunny day, near freezing in the morning. My Ranger got dented in the ferry line at Mukilteo at 10:24am. Some Oriental woman opened her door against my driver's side rear fender. She said she was sorry after I started to get out. Her door scraped a little paint off and left a small dent. I think her partner was a white man and they had a large brown lab dog. Patched garage roof north side.

10-31-99 Ferry fare reduced in October to $4.00. State still working on new Clinton Ferry dock. Ferries have to use the north landing so it is quite peaceful on the beach.

11-28-99 Rain can is full again. We are above normal in rainfall this month. I had Thanksgiving alone. Marian brought me a pumpkin pie on their way to dinner. My neighbors in Kent gave me a plate of turkey dinner. It looks like a young couple with a little boy and 2 dogs are living in Carol's house! I still haven't drained the pipes.

12-19-99 I wrote to LeeRoy Young and he updated me on current events. The large friendly rabbit was adopted and taken back to the mainland. Carol moved to Anchorage. Diane is going to come back up and live in her house next door to me. The weather is miserable up here today, rain and fog.

1-19-2000 We had a strong windstorm a couple days ago. 300,000 households were out of power. My power was out here and 3 hours in Kent.

1-29-2000 Super weather today although it was 28 in the morning. I put some temporary aluminum roof patches on the bathroom and utility room roofs.

2-12-2000 Getting quite a few dog poops in my yard. I think Diane's kids have some dogs.

4-8-2000 I still haven't turned on water. There are a bunch of kids in Diane's house. The Deer Lake drain is washing out our clam beds. I think Lindfors has diverted it to our beach. My tulips are doing good.

4-22-2000 I turned on the cold water. I adjusted the new toilet shut off. I had to turn on the water because they were having an Easter egg hunt at the park so I could not use the outhouse. My electric range indicator light has stayed on for a couple weeks though the burners are not on!

5-2-2000 My long distance eyesight is out of focus lately. I'm staying overnight for the 1st time this year. French's cancelled Easter dinner this year due to lack of interest. My Kent neighbors brought over a nice piping hot Easter plate. It consisted of roast beef, salmon filet, jelly bean cake, asparagus. I made 3 meals out of it. I'm the only one putting flowers on Lucille's grave.

5-21-2000 Whirlpool indicator light still on all the time. I was very sick to my stomach at Kent a few days ago. Got sick eight times. I had made meatballs from hamburger, pork, parmesan cheese, milk, egg and bread. I also used some garlic chips. I'm not positive that the meatballs were the culprit.

6-17-2000 Beautiful day today 76 degrees. The neighbors to the north had all their kids up this weekend. They brought 4 dogs! They keep a pretty close watch on them. I was kinda worried about all the dog poop but Diane brought me some fresh cooked crab so what could I say after that kindness. They have cleared their beach of a lot of logs and they have quite a few beach fires. I filled the hot water tank, it hasn't been used since the New Year's Eve 1996 mudslide. I haven't turned on the electricity to the tank yet. I've been getting by with using kettle boiled water to do the dishes and wash hands. I crawled under the cabin and put an 8" x 16" patio block under N/W bedroom corner pier. I drilled a hole in north garage wall preparing to raise it a little. I painted the cabin skirting bottom row of shingles.

6-30-2000 I put another pier under the west bedroom. There is a huge run of Sockeye salmon this year. The Indians say we can have a Sockeye season this year but not in time for the fourth of July. I replaced another pier under the east wall.

7-23-2000 Bought 2 more patio blocks and placed them under the pier at the south west corner of the west bedroom. The pier had shifted a few inches because of the 1996 New Year's Eve mud slide. Bud is 80 years old this year. Sandee had a barbeque for him on July 22. Bud walks with a cane now.

8-12-2000 I straightened the north garage wall a little more with the farm jack and hoist. I still have a lot more to do. The hanging light switch in the guest bedroom has quit working. It looks like it got pretty hot, it's about 50 years old. The indicator light for the surface burners on the Whirlpool range still stays on all the time. I came up during the week because I figured nobody in the house north of me would be home but there is always somebody there. Some of her kids were there this time.

9-7-2000 I pulled the north wall of the shed up a little straighter.

I'm going to have to rearrange the prop timbers before I proceed any further.

9-17-2000 I bought 2 8x10 tarps from Fred Meyer for $5.95 each. They are not as good as the last ones. They have fewer grommets. I used them on the Skagit (boat). The Firestone Tire Company has sold millions of defective tires for their light trucks and S.U.V. vehicles. They are recalling them. My Ranger pickup muffler has a hole in it. I covered the hole with a piece of steel and an aeroseal clamp.

10-1-2000 I straightened the north wall of the garage 4 more inches. We had an inch of rain this week. The Mariners are in the playoffs. The Silver run was huge this fall. The state is allowing a 6 fish limit in Lake Washington. The Whirlpool range burner warning light still stays on all the time. My Ranger muffler has a hole in it. I have 36,000 on the truck, I had a new muffler put in at 17,000 at Lifetime Muffler.

10-29-2000 Sandy stopped to say hello as she walked by. Sandy communicates with Bonnie and Bud by email. Bud's memory is failing, he's 80 years old. He also has an intestinal aneurism. Bonnie has quit golf to take care of Bud. I dug up some of the tulips and transplanted them. The beach has really changed. There is a large spit building up in front of my neighbors to the north. My Starling barricade on the roof has pulled loose. The Ranger passed its emission test.

11-25-2000 I came for the last time before the state remodels the Mukilteo Ferry dock. After the 27th the car ferry will have to go to Edmonds. It is rainy and windy today but I still had to come up and check on things. My neighbors cut up their beach logs and now we are beginning to lose sand. I didn't turn on the water this time.

1-6-2001 1st time up in the new millennium. Quite foggy on the trip up. The state is still working on the Mukilteo dock. Some Boy Scouts picked up some Fir tree limbs that I had stacked by the side of the road, that was their good deed.

1-20-2001 Came up to check property after the highest tides in 14 years. We were lucky because the winds were not very high so the beach is OK. My Ranger truck needs a new muffler at 36,000 and this will be its second one.

2-11-2001 The weatherman said it was going to snow today but he missed the boat. It turned out to be a beautiful sunny day. Our beach has really changed since I was here last. The big hole is all filled up with sand.

2-24-2001 Had a very dry winter. Everybody is supposed to conserve electricity and water. The reservoirs are the lowest in history.

4-21-2001 I turned on my cold water for the first time this year. The gardener hit my brand new boat trailer license plate with his lawnmower and bent it badly. I was so proud of that new license number "2020NB". I haven't even shown it off out on the road, now he has ruined it. I may fire him.

6-23-2001 I stopped my mail beginning on Friday June 22. I wanted to be up here to protect my clam bed. My neighbors to the north had their clan up on 6-23. They had about 15 people! They dug a lot of clams but they respected my beach fairly well. They had a large barbeque and played the accordion. They also had a bonfire in their new fire-pit and sat around it till midnight. The situation is quite different than when Carol rented the house. Speaking of Carol, she was in a horrible auto accident this weekend in Alaska and was killed. Toot Young was the one who told me about Carol's death and LeeRoy Young gave me an internet printout of the Alaska newspaper article. That is really speedy news using the Internet, he is way ahead of me on his computer. Lucille used to have long chats with Carol.

7-8-2001 I've been coming up early Sunday mornings because that is about the only time there is a slight pause in traffic jams. Sometimes I can make it up to Mukilteo in 55 minutes. I'm still repairing mud slide damage that happened 4 years ago.

7-19-2001 Came up during the week for a change to check the

beach on a -3.3 tide. I had the whole beach to myself, nobody was digging.

8-5-2001 I'm still working on the 1997 mud slide damage. Maridel hasn't called in 8 months and I haven't seen Chris in 3 years. I thought I'd have some privacy by staying during the weekdays but my north neighbor's relatives showed up on Monday. It looks like they are staying overnight.

8-19-2001 Mr. Tasche fell off a ladder and broke his ankle. He was working on his daughter's house. Neighbors to the north had their property surveyed and the distance between the north face of Tasche's wall (neighbor on the south) and the survey stake on the north neighbor's lot line is only 49'4". So one of them is trying to take 8.09 inches of my property.

9-16-2001 The weather is grey with fog and drizzle. On Sept 11, 2001 the Muslim terrorists attached the World Trade Center and the Pentagon. We might go to war over this. Rescuers are trying to recover the bodies, but it is very difficult. The pile of twisted steel at the World Trade Center is 7 stories high.

10-14-2001 I planted a tulip bulb, a very dark one. It is extremely foggy this morning until noon. I haven't heard that many fog horns in a long time.

11-10-2001 Drained hot water tank. Planted "Orange Emperor Tulip".

12-8-2001 3' of rain in the rain gauge. I had to drive in some snow showers coming up. Another mudslide occurred behind my neighbors to the south and some smaller ones to the north. I have a website now. I signed in on Nov. 28, 2001.

12-23-2001 Rain gauge filled again. I sent my first email to LeeRoy Young on 12-15-2001, he replied on the same day. I sent one to Bonnie and she replied. I sent the third one to the French's, they have not replied. Maridel never phoned me all this year! Today has been cold and clear, 32 degrees, rain had been predicted.

1-25-2002 Came up for a quick check up. There is supposed to be a cold snap coming with some snow. I guess Allan had some slight strokes last Saturday. Bud needs oxygen to keep going.

3-24-2002 My tulips are coming up good. I fertilized them with bulb& bloom food. The Deer Lake drain is still ravaging our beach. Most of the pilings for the new dock have been driven on the Clinton Dock extension. Someone cut a 100' Cottonwood tree that was on my beach into shorter pieces. That was quite a worrisome tree. They also cut a fresh Fir tree log on my beach.

4-20-2002 Jim (neighbor to the north) was the one who cut up the 100' Cottonwood. Now we have another one even longer. I wacked some dandelions with a sickle. I haven't turned on the water yet. LeeRoy sent me a photo by email of my cabin. M. French sent me a photo of Chris's family by email. A crow was building a nest in my shed, I had to remove it.

5-4-2002 The Deer Lake drain is still flowing through my beach. I think the neighbors to the north have started to cut a trench on my beach because their beach and Young's beach are eroding worse than mine. I don't appreciate that. I turned on the cold water for the first time this year. I also spun the boat trailer wheels to circulate the wheel bearing grease. I rode my bicycle to the end of the road. Ferry fare is $6.20 now.

6-15-2002 The Montgomery clan (neighbors to the north) is up this weekend for father's Day. They are quite the beach fire bunch, so if the wind is from the north the smoke gets sort of aggravating. The Deer Lake drain still has our beaches messed up. I got a nice card from the French's.

6-29-2002 Montgomery's kids are up here with their little white dog. They burned in their fire pit, north wind. They have two boys about 12 years old. A robin has a nest with an egg in my garage. Sheriff lectured me in the ferry line for traveling too long in the line. I straightened a post jack that tilted because of the 1996 slide. It was under the living room.

9-21-2002 Tacked a few shingles on the north porch ridge.

Pumped up boat trailer tires and put 8x16 cement blocks under the tires. A lot of people say this has been the best summer weather in a long time.

10-19-2002 Scraped moss off shed room, extreme fog has engulfed the area overnight. It is 11:00 am and the fog persists.

11-2-2002 The weather has been freezing for about a week at night. I lost my Dahlias in Kent. We have had the driest October since 1948.

11-16-2002 Came up after a major wind and rain storm. I now own a couple hundred more logs. The neighbors to the north have very few logs after the storm. Young's have a little dog now. They had a new septic tank in the front yard

12-21-2002 Hundreds more logs on my beach. The Deer Lake drain is roaring. We have a big lake on our beaches. Flooding in Snohomish County. High winds and high tides have really made a mess. It's a good thing I'm done fishing.

1-5-2003 A terrible series of storms and high tides has devastated my beach. I now own about 1,000 new logs. One good thing did occur, the Deer Lake drain changed course. The drain made a sharp right turn and is eroding my neighbor's beach. The drain no longer reaches up to me.

Well he is not exaggerating - there must be a thousand logs on the beach. If those logs had been there when I moved the cottage down here, I never could have dragged it across the beach to where it now sits. Those logs will remain there for another 15 years until they rot and until the folks with cabins on the beach finally chainsaw them all up making paths to the beach. One good storm and those cut-up logs will float away.

2-1-2003 The space shuttle blew up this morning!! The shuttle was named the Columbia!!! My thousands of beach logs did not leave, in fact we gained more. There is a dead seal on the beach in front of Tasches (south) place. Vessels are not allowed within 500 yards of the ferries now for fear of terrorism.

3-29-2003 Turned on cold water, meter read 19,750. LeeRoy showed me an article about Berte Olson (the former owner of our cabin). I drove up to Langley to the newspaper to try and get a copy of that article, but they were closed. My tulip bed is flourishing. I used my new cell phone Nokia Model 5185i for the first time up here. My old Nokia 211 purchased in 1996 is off the charts, I couldn't find a battery for it. I purchased the new one on the day the 2nd Iraq war started. The war is still raging. There is a lot of security on the ferries for fear of terrorists nowadays the state patrol looks everybody over and the Coast Guard sometimes escorts the ferries.

4-12-2003 The Gray whales swimming in front of the ferry on the trip over this morning had all the tourists excited. The whales have been around south Whidbey for a couple of weeks. My tulips are really doing great in my little tulip bed.

5-10-2003 Ranger now has 43,000 on the odometer. The Iraq War is over. The aircraft carrier Abraham Lincoln has returned to Everett after a 10 month tour. The crew was given a ticker tape parade by 30,000 citizens today!

5-24-2003 I stopped the mail and paper for this 3 day holiday. All the logs are still stacked up and I thought I would be OK walking on them. The logs were wet, I had on my trusty lineman's boots and a walking stick, but I didn't get very far before I slipped and fell! I wrenched my left knee, bumped my tail bone and hit my head so hard my ears rang, then I crossed a few more logs and fell again! I'm not going to walk on wet logs any more, I hope nobody saw me. The neighbors to the north are bringing up all kinds of junk from the home they just sold in town. They look like worse packrats than I am. My gardener hit the bottom step on my south porch with his lawn mower. So far he has broke the step, bent my new boat trailer license plate, and broke the legs on the picnic table.

6-7-2003 I brought up another 12"x12" pier block from Dunn Lumber. It cost $2.98. I worked under the cabin in the 90 degree heat. I've been crawling under the cabin trying to prop up the north porch steps.

7-6-2003 Came up to see how many fireworks were on my property. So far I've only noticed one or two. I put a 4x4 post under the north porch. My left hand feels like it is starting to become paralyzed after driving up here. This happens every once in a while.

8-16-2003 Montgomery's house (north neighbor) has been torn down! Excavators cut a 6" root from my fir tree that had encroached onto the Montgomery property. I don't have a full 50.09' between Tasches bulkhead and Montgomery's chalk line. The two neighbors are trying to squeeze me and leave me with only 49'. So I figure I own one of their concrete walls! Montgomery had his property surveyed, but Tasche did not have his surveyed! The Langley Fair had a tragedy on Aug 16th. A ride owner got caught in the machinery and was killed.

8-30-2003 The Montgomery's foundation has been poured. They also put a wall along our property line. The Tasche's on my south side had a huge gathering of 25-50 people. They had music playing all day. We have had 52 days of dry weather, never below 70 degrees! I don't have to worry about being noisy because both north and south neighbors have been making plenty.

10-25-2003 We had an all time record rainfall for one day on Oct. 20. Many areas had over 5 inches! Most rivers flooded and all the log debris has come across to Columbia Beach, as if we didn't already have a surplus. The extreme rainfall caused my 2nd Skagit boat tarp to rip apart. Nobody called me.

11-8-2003 Came up to see moon eclipse, really get a good view up here. A surprise wind storm from the N.W. damaged Ivar's Restaurant at Mukilteo.

11-22-2003 I'm 80 now. We've had snow up here. My boat tarp has caved in with ice. I put more antifreeze in toilet and traps. Builders have been parking in my yard.

12-20-2003 I put tar paper over bathroom. French's are going to San Francisco to see Chris and Kim for Xmas. I'm here all alone.

My goodness! Wil is 80 years of age and he is up on the roof in December putting tar paper over the bathroom and he is there all alone.

2-7-2004 My temporary roofing paper tarp over the bathroom blew partly off. Nobody called! Some of my iron pipe insulation disintegrated and fell off the attic pipe to the kitchen sink. I haven't figured out how many pipes burst in the January freeze. I'll wait til the weather warms up.

3-6-2004 Montgomery's house construction vehicles have made big ruts in my yard. My tulips are coming up. I fertilized tulips. Nice sunny day today. I still haven't turned on my water. I hope I don't have too many burst pipes. Since all the neighbors built their mansions they caused my taxes to be over $3,000 this year!

5-1-2004 A freak storm blew a bunch more shingles off my west wing and my poor storage shed! The neighbors with tin roofs survived the storm without worrying about shingles. Gas is over $2.00 per gallon! I stayed overnight for the first time this year. I still haven't fixed the bathroom sink supply pipe washers so I can't use the sink. I'm still trying to restore my plumbing damaged by the freeze in January. The hot water faucet in the kitchen sink split wide open. I'm wasting a lot of time on plumbing. I wish I had not forgotten to drain those pipes. Gas is $2.30 per gallon.

6-12-2004 The power went off after I've only been here for 2 hours. I didn't turn on the water and I guess I won't stay overnight. Montgomery starts his motor home generator (they are staying in a motor home on their property while their home is being built). President Reagan's funeral was yesterday.

6-26-2004 Lyle, my co-worker and bowling buddy passed away on June 21. He was married 56 years. I'm still trying to stop the bathroom sink supply lines from leaking after the cold water supply line burst out of its connecting nut because of the January 2004 freeze.

7-9-2004 My Fir tree is turning brown, I think the neighbors killed it. People are still trying to burn my cottage down. I found a rocket on my roof.

7-25-2004 My insurance company won't renew my Whidbey Homeowner policy. My agent arranged to change insurance company for the Whidbey property. The new company is Foremost Insurance Company. They cancelled my policy on Aug 21. I had paid the first quarter premium of $105.00, they gave it back and dumped me. So now I don't have any insurance on Whidbey!

8-15-2004 I've been crawling under the cabin trying to prepare a sturdier base for my wobbling toilet. The weather has been very warm and dry this summer. Over twenty 80 degree days.

What did I tell you? He is over 80 years old and still crawling under the cottage in that cramped, wet, cold space to repair a toilet. Don't know why he doesn't call a repairman now. He doesn't need to do those things himself anymore. Just doesn't want to spend the money I guess.

10-10-2004 State Patrol dog sniffed my truck at Mukilteo. The Iraq terrorists have everybody worried just before the presidential election. I turned on the hot water heater for the first time this year. I still haven't fixed the hot water supply line on the bathroom sink. I'm trying to design a stronger foundation for the bathroom toilet, it wobbles quite a bit now. Mr. Young is installing a metal carport for his new truck. Mt. St. Helens is having numerous earthquakes and small eruptions today.

10-23-2004 Scraped moss off of outbuilding and SW part of cottage. Put a "No Admittance" sign on north porch steps. Addie Grims talked to me. She pities me and wants the Island Habitat for Humanity volunteers to come and restore my cottage and outbuilding.

11-6-2004 One side of the roofing paper over the bathroom came loose, lucky thing I came up because it is raining today. Jim Tasche, my neighbor to the south never even called me about the problem! I put some new insulation on the attic pipes. The old style insulation had deteriorated to become a sticky worthless mess. Gas is $2.02 per gallon. President Bush has been re-elected.

11-20-2004 My mailbox in Kent was damaged and vandals threw my mail in the road in the rain. I still haven't drained the pipes. The Montgomery's finally moved their view-blocking motor home. It was blocking my view of oncoming traffic.

12-18-2004 My roofing paper blew off the roof again. I dropped my voice box when I got to Kent last time. I had to have it repaired down in Vancouver. I was without a voice for a week!

1-29-2005 Mr. Montgomery has gotten a bid from a tree surgeon to take my tree down! He is willing to pay half of the cost which is $560.00! I haven't signed the contract yet, but probably will because the neighbors hate the tree and me. I was going to talk to him today but he is having a huge paving job done around his house and he is not around. The trucks are tearing up my yard.

3-12-2005 Turned on cold water. LeeRoy Young wants me to walk to the beach by using his ramp instead of walking over all my logs. Aircraft carrier has just returned to Everett after saving the Sri Lanka tsunami victims from starving. A statewide water shortage has been declared by our new governor.

3-27-2005 Came up on Easter Sunday. I washed the dinghy in a rainstorm so I didn't deplete the critical water supply. The wind blew my roofing paper off the bathroom roof last night. I had to stop my other maintenance problems and tack on some more roofing paper.

4-9-2005 I tacked a few shingles on the outbuilding. Toot Young came over and pleaded with me to cut my Noble Spruce tree down because the tree's needles bothered them so much. She is recovering from knee surgery. I told her that I will contact the tree surgeon as soon as the weather dries the property out. Security officers are still sniffing the automobiles in the ferry line. Gas is $2.42 per gallon.

6-4-2005 Toot Young has been diagnosed with breast cancer. Montgomery's son's big dog would not let me get to my truck. I put some bricks under the north porch bottom step.

6-22-2005 Came up to check the clam bed on a -3.9 tide. Tasche's Whidbey relatives had started a driftwood log fort on my property. Their Dakota relatives really enlarged the fort. I don't know why these people with their fancy manicured property can't do all this fort building on their own property. I'm self-insured and these people left me with this dangerous mess and fled. Gas is $2.22 per gallon.

7-20-2005 Came up during the week to keep an eye on my clam bed on a -3.5 tide. The moon was beautiful. Nobody was digging clams. Most of the log fort on my beach has been dismantled. A new fort has been built on Montgomery's beach. The London subway has been bombed by the Muslims. 55 people killed. Food is being served on the ferries again.

8-6-2005 Now the Montgomery's have put up a white vinyl trellis that is blocking my view of Mt. Baker. After I was kind enough to have my view blocking spruce removed they turn around and immediately block my view. Kim and Chris moved back from San Francisco to Kirkland. Chris hasn't spoken to me since Aug. 1, 1999!

8-20-2005 There are about 50 people at Montgomery's today! They were so busy cooking and drinking that they didn't notice Jim's boat started drifting away. I had to run over and warn him. Then to top everything off on this Saturday, the neighbor to the south is having his house re-roofed!! The roofing company started at 11:00 am. They have been banging and scraping all day. The homeowners fled the scene. I guess these roofers are going to keep on until dusk. The Montgomery's have loud music in addition to all their jabbering. I don't belong here anymore.

I'm so sad to hear him say that he doesn't belong here anymore. He has had this fishing cottage for 50 years now. He is all alone and the world is changing. It no longer is what he has always known. Where is the place he knew so well? Where does he find peace and contentment? He has no one to talk it all over with, these feelings of anger, resentment and feeling lost. The feeling that he doesn't belong anymore. He has cut himself off from relatives and friends and he is also of the age where those few friends he might have kept are leaving because they are sick and/or dying. I think he is retreating and letting the world pass him by. He can see what is happening but doesn't know how to be heard, or even what he might say, so he stays quiet and just watches as if it is a world separate from the one he lives in, the one he 'belongs' in.

7-19-2005 Another old-time house has been torn down and another huge house is going to be built there. LeeRoy Young said his daughter would really like to buy my cottage if I ever should decide to sell.

9-25-2005 I brought up the 8' stepladder. It's a lot easier to check on the roofs with the 8-footer. I took Lucille's bike down to Kent.

10-8-2005 Diane Montgomery's son sent me a letter of intent from Las Vegas. He has offered to buy my cottage, so he can live near Diane and Jim. He has always admired my cottage. He says he will take care of the taxes and insurance.

12-18-2005 Bud passed away on Dec. 8 at a Health and Rehab Center in Montesano, WA. I came up to check the pipes. We've had a very cold and dry December.

2-5-2006 A terrible windstorm occurred yesterday. The storm from the south west moved a huge amount of my logs to the north onto Montgomery's property. It blew my roofing paper off the bathroom, it is a good thing I came up. I'm missing the Super Bowl. My beach has changed completely.

2-11-2006 I have a little better access to the beach now after the Feb 4 storm. The Deer Lake drain now goes straight out from where it dumps into the sound. I've always wished it would do that so it wouldn't come north through my beach.

6-17-2006 Pruned shrubs. Got a Father's Day card from French's. Sharon the Census interviewer gave me my last interview yesterday.

7-2-2006 My ferry fare was free on 7/2/06! Somebody donated some ferry fares!! That is the first time in 50 years that has ever happened to me!! I turned on the hot water for the first time this year! I got to try out the new Globe valve that I installed on 4/22/06. The Montgomery's are having another huge family gathering including all their huge dogs. I'm hosing down my cedar roof to protect it from the usual fireworks. Montgomery's gave me a huge cooked crab on the 4th of July. Jim said they had some extra. I watched the fireworks. The Columbia Beach residents really put on a show to rival Everett's big show.

7-15-2006 They are digging up our road in Kent to put in sewers for the two huge museum homes. I came up to get away from all the noise and dust. I'm removing the old shingles from over the bathroom. Jim Tasche is selling his house.

9-3-2006 The Jim Tasche family has moved. Montgomery's had a large gathering for Labor Day with all their kids, dogs and beach fires.

10-7-2006 I left my flashlight on the south porch for 2 weeks, nobody took it. I'm using a gel pen to see if the ink doesn't fade. Mt. Rainier had a 4.5 earthquake on 10/7.

12-2-2006 November has been the wettest in Seattle history!! 15.6"!! I have the 8'x16' tarp on the west wing, one of the 12"x12" stepping stones blew off or slid off and crashed down on my classic picnic table. The picnic table collapsed. The stepping stone and 4 cement bricks blew off or slid off.

1-20-2007 The weather has been so snowy and windy and wet this is the 1st chance I've been able to come up and check the tarps. Now I have to dash back to Kent because the developers are closing in on me!

2-17-2007 Finally a sunny day, for a few minutes. I guess Maridel has bought a home in Guadalajara. The Deer lake drain is roaring but it does not come my way. I still have tons of logs.

5-31-2007 I came up during the week because the weather was unpleasant on the Memorial Day weekend. As soon as I arrived the Montgomery's and the new neighbors to the south of me departed. LeeRoy Young celebrated his 80th birthday.

6-16-2007 Came up to see the beach on a -3.6 tide. Nobody was digging. The local people had already dug during the week. Last week at my Kent residence the development company started a miserable 8 unit housing project with cheap little road right adjacent to my back fence line! Gas is $2.99.

8-11-2007 Today a new roof was nailed on the west half of the cabin.

9-26-2007 Put new license plate on the boat trailer. The new numbers are 4123UB. I don't know why the DOL sent the new plate, my old one wasn't very old and I really liked it. I had a new hot tar roof put on the Kent house, it cost $24,065.03. Quite foggy up here this time. Roofs have cost me $30,000 this year!

11-3-2007 Drained the hot water tank. Gas is $3.20 per gallon. My computer in Kent has a message that blocks me from going on the Internet. It has been blocked since August. Nobody calls me, I don't know any family news. Messages are stacking up on the computer but I have no way to read them or answer. Technicians say I must upgrade or get a newer computer! Draining the tank took 50 minutes.

2-3-2008 Shoveled mud out of driveway. Super Bowl today.

4-5-2008 Came up to shovel landslide mud, but my new neighbor on the south has shoveled all my mud for me!

5-17-2008 The picture I took of Toot and Roy with my Polaroid camera appeared in the South Whidbey Record Saturday May 17, 2008, Vol 84, No. 40 page A12. Toot and Roy used the old picture to invite friends to their 60th wedding anniversary gathering at Holmes Harbor Rod and Gun Club. I got in a wreck with the Ranger. She bumped into me with a Chev Astro Van. The accident happened at 2;20 PM. My Ranger has a damaged left rear panel, a damaged left rear wheel, a burned out bulb and a bent axle.

9-14-2008 Came up in the Probe for the first time since May. I had catarack (cataract) surgery on my right eye on Sept 2. I see quite a bit better now. A motor cyclist stole a battery off of Montgomery's vacation trailer yesterday. My Kent neighbors were burglarized last week.

9-28-2008 The Ranger is still not repaired. The country is going into an economic meltdown. WAMU bank has been purchased by JP Morgan. WAMU's stock went from $45.00 to .50 cents.

11-5-2008 I haven't been up for quite a while. My two eye doctors tell me I have a hole in my retina that will require surgery. I have a defect of the retina in my right eye but I may not need surgery. I've been examined by about 8 eye doctors.

2-5-2009 Checked cottage. Contractor still putting rocks on the bank to the west of my two south neighbors. It's a huge project to control the mudslides.

4-5-2009 First day of 70 degrees since last October. I fell down the south porch steps and hit my head on Peterson's concrete wall (south neighbor). My head bled quite a bit. I turned on the cold water for the first time this year.

This is a preview of things to come for Wil. Not long from now, (4 years), in 2011 Wil falls and hits his head again, this time at his Kent house. He is taken to the hospital and the hospital staff are not able to locate any next-of-kin. That's when Wil becomes a "ward of the state" and is appointed a guardian. That is also the event that starts the sale of his "belongings" - his Kent house and his Whidbey fishing cottage while Wil is put in an old-folks home. Pretty sad if you ask me.

4-19-2009 We are in the midst of a depression. Thousands of people are being laid off across the nation. The rock retaining wall on the west side of the road behind my south neighbors is still in progress. I rode my bike on April 19.

5-3-2009 A Swine flu epidemic is spreading around the world. It started in Mexico. Schools are closing, people are afraid to fly to Mexico. Many people wear masks. The Montgomery's and their son have just cut a path through the beach logs between my place and theirs so I can get to the beach now. They worry about me crawling over the logs.

5-19-2009 The recession is still with us. Auto dealerships are being forced to close. Schools are laying off teachers. I'm a little incontinent. I'm using Depends for Men. Some hoodlum opened my Kent mailbox and put the flag up on 5/17.

5-31-2009 The deadline to switch to digital TV is near. GM has gone bankrupt on June 1. I'm starting to drink coffee again. I went to visit Lucille's grave on Memorial Day.

6-14-2009 I turned on the hot water tank for the first time this year! We haven't had any rain for about 30 days. I don't get a good enough signal to use my Radio Shack converter box, so I don't get the digital programs that became mandatory on June 12.

7-12-2009 A man jumped off the Cathlamet ferry last night on the 12:30am run. It rained yesterday at last. Peterson children gave me some raspberries. Glazed cottage windows. Driest July on record, supposed to be in the nineties all week!

8-23-2009 Working on support for the toilet. Stayed longer than usual. Still a lot of boaters this late in the year even being in a recession.

10-24-2009 Rainy season has started. The country is in 2 wars and a recession, and we are preparing for a Swine flu epidemic, there is a shortage of flu medicine. A lot of flu victims are dying.

11-12-2009 Drained hot water tank. I fell out of bed and cut my forehead. My lawn still has not been cut.

1-10-2010 Changed 9V battery in the smoke detector. Put water in refrigerator freezer trays. 50 degrees in cabin.

10-15-2010 Came up for the first time in several months. The Kittitas has broke down.

You just read the last entry Wil ever made. October 15, 2010 was probably the very last time Wil visited his beloved fishing cottage. He had no idea on that day that he would not be returning and thus left everything in place, as if he would return in a month or two. That is how I found the cottage in March of 2012 (minus a few items that had been taken by persons unknown). The cottage sat empty for 1.5 years. The gentle man with no voice was gone.

On a separate piece of lined paper, tucked in the back of the 4th journal, Wil wrote the following:

My cottage was barged here from Deception Pass about 1940. The owner was Berte Olsen, the first female ferry boat captain on Puget Sound.

My outbuilding took the brunt of a mudslide on New Year's Day 1997. The outbuilding was moved 17 inches, the cottage was also bumped by a tree and shifted about 6 inches.

Six months after the slide, surgeons performed a laryngectomy on my throat and removed my voice box.

Six months after that my wife passed away.

Wil's presence is still in the cottage. Among the feelings noticed in the cottage is a very sad and lonely male presence. I know that presence is Wil. He often guided me in the work I did on the cottage. Many times I would find just the right tool or needed part amongst his collection of things for a repair I was preparing to do. I know he is pleased at the restoration of the cottage. I hope that being amongst the joy and happy life that happens now in the cottage, he is able to find peace and happiness again. I had hoped to meet him one day, but that was not to be.

I believe that Wil and Berte sit side-by-side at the kitchen window looking out at the Salish Sea with a peaceful contentment on their faces. There is no place they would rather be.

18 CHANGE WITHIN THE CONTEXT OF LIFE

In life, the one constant, inevitable and guaranteed event is change. It is often feared, emotion-filled and even painful because it involves letting go of the present and of certain visions or dreams that were held for the future. We constantly imagine the future - what we will be doing, who we will be with, where we will be in our careers, our living circumstances, our relationships, and our leisure time activities. Sometimes our visions and dreams are brought to reality and sometimes they are not, or at least not in the same way we envisioned them. I had a vision for the cottage. I knew what it looked like and what it felt like.

I lived that vision and dream for four years. Wonderful times sitting on the patio in the late afternoon enjoying the fresh-caught Dungeness crab that had been brought in just hours before. Friends, family and I would be sitting in the sunshine, sharing stories and laughing with one another as juice from the succulent crab dribbled down our arms. The sweet flavor of the crab was exceeded only by the sweetness of the moment shared with those people I love dearly. So many adventures are vivid in my mind, the crabbing, boating, digging clams, walking the beach, restoring and maintaining the cottage and sitting around the fire-pit with friends and family. They were my vision and dream come true. How blessed I feel.

I believed those memorable times would continue into my future for at least a decade or two. I held that vision and so did my friends and family. Until it changed.

I sold the cottage last week, just four years after it came to be mine. It was something I did not think I would be doing nearly this soon as I love the little cottage dearly. Life has a way of happening and interrupting those dreams. Actually I do not think of it as an "interruption", I think of it as my "next dream". In the context of life, it is all good and with a positive belief for the future, changes lead to an even more abundant and joyful life.

"Life is either a daring adventure or nothing at all". Helen Keller

I am 67 years old now and taking care of two houses is challenging. That was the easy answer to why I was selling the cottage. It was a lot to manage, to say nothing of the fact that energy is now a finite commodity where once I thought I had endless energy. It was obvious to me that I needed to consolidate into one home and live there full time. Of course it would be the cottage I would keep, but that proved to be difficult for a variety of reasons.

If I were to make this my primary home for the next 20 years it would require bringing my yard up to the level of the elevated yards on each side of mine and adding a cement bulkhead along the beach as each of them has done. That meant importing hundreds of yards of "certified" fill dirt. A very expensive proposition and not in keeping with the size and value of the little cottage. If I wanted to avoid being dwarfed by 2 and 3-story houses I would have to tear the cottage down and replace it with a new, big house, one in keeping with the escalating property values on the beach and the houses on each side of mine. I could not do that, I loved the cottage and its' history too much. I had worked so hard to restore all that was there while preserving the original cottage that had been loved so dearly by Wil.

There was another issue at play as well. My recognition of this issue took some honest, self-reflection. I listened to my thoughts as well as what I shared with others during the last year I owned the cottage. I was getting frustrated and angry. That realization surprised me. Wil had become angry at circumstances and people for "ruining" his enjoyment of the little cottage. I was sounding like Wil!

The issues involving water drainage will always plague the little cottage as it sits lower than the neighboring houses. The three-story house to the south of the cottage will always block the sunshine for much of the day in winter. The re-grading of the road in front of the cottage that made the garage useless would always be that high. The relationships with the immediate neighbors hadn't turned out as I had hoped and I was disappointed. I realized that just like Wil, these things were bubbling up negative thoughts within me. The feelings of anger and frustration would surface when I was in the cottage and that was new to me. I don't like living in negativity. I was saddened and I was not happy with myself. This flew in the face of who I believe I am. It was also not how I choose to live my life. I was losing interest and joy in being at the cottage. It used to fill my heart with openness and gladness. I had a piece of beach and beach life. Now there was an uncomfortable "edge" to being at the cottage.

Through his journals I could see what Wil's negative thoughts had done to him, his enjoyment of the cottage and his life. I would not let that happen to me. One of my lessons learned in this life is that if I am not happy with what is, it is up to me and me alone to change in order for things to be different and (hopefully) better.

Doing the same thing over and over again and expecting different results is Albert Einstein's definition of insanity.

Relationships with neighbors can be tenuous and disappointing. Sometimes there is just nothing you can do about it. They can also be filled with warm and caring interactions that lead to wonderful friendships and memorable times. I needed to move the negativity out of my life and focus on the positive. Positive was the relationship with Toot and Roy, my neighbors one house to the north. Whenever Toot saw me in the yard of the cottage she would lean out her door and yell "Hey Sue, come on over!" She was such a positive, happy person and together with her husband LeeRoy (Roy), we had wonderful afternoons sitting together, telling tales of the beach and gazing out at the water and all the activity that is Columbia Beach. Roy died two years into that friendship and he is greatly missed. I believe he still sits alongside Toot as we regularly sit up against her picture windows, chatting up a storm while gazing out over the beach we love so well.

A positive attitude and happiness is my responsibility. To stay negative and unhappy with current circumstances and change something to improve those circumstances is to choose the negative and be unhappy. I may choose to be unhappy, but I also need to own that. There are people who believe their unhappiness is caused by someone else, or is someone else's fault. That is not taking responsibility. When I admit responsibility, it puts the solution into my hands, gives me the power to change and I become not the victim but rather the creator. I definitely choose to be happy.

Of course there are some things you can't change. The serenity prayer says it beautifully - *God grant me the Serenity to accept the things I cannot change, Courage to change the things I can and Wisdom to know the difference.* How you react to those things you cannot change is what you have the power to change. In other words, what I could change was how I felt and what I would do about it.

Even though I longed for the relationships I used to have with my sisters, I had to acknowledge that people change because the world and our circumstances change. This was an example of something I wanted to be the way it was before - before kids, before mom's death, before jobs, before change. I wish that I saw my children more often, that they would stop by for dinner or a chat but we are on our own individual journeys. We have priorities and lifestyles that have shaped and changed us and all is just as it should be. I have learned to be at peace with that, even if the reality is not the vision I held for so long.

All that said and carefully considered, I knew it was time to make a change in my circumstances but I didn't know exactly what that meant. Did change mean destroying the cottage and putting up a large home, equal to the two on either side of the cottage? Did change mean abandoning what I had worked so hard to build and what my vision of the future was built around? Did change mean giving up a dream? I asked a lot of questions, made many financial calculations and did a lot of thinking. It was hard and painful but I arrived at the decision that I had to let the cottage go. Letting go meant selling it. I put the cottage on the market to be sold 4 years and 3 months after I bought it .

Some of my friends, family and neighbors have not understood why I let it go. Many thought it was merely an investment from the beginning. I admit it was never a bad investment, but it was something entirely different than that for me. It and all the people connected to me and to the cottage provided a lovely adventure, a sweet experience in life and a beautiful memory that will live on forever in my heart and mind. Me staying there was not to be, for financial, social and emotional reasons. It was time to move on.

I have now stepped into a new adventure, a segue onto a new path for my life which will bring new learning and I am not sure exactly what else. I am building a new house, on the bluff overlooking Columbia Beach, just 20 cabins down from the little cottage I loved and so enjoyed. I am building the dream home I've always had in my mind and heart. A home that emerges from my desire and creativity, suits my needs and houses me comfortably well into my future. Thus far, building a house has been a fantastic journey across a long and bumpy road. I had no idea about most of the challenges I would encounter, and there have been many. I know I will look back and say it was a very rewarding journey.

The decision to sell the cottage was mine and mine alone. To my surprise (and perhaps I should not have been surprised at all) my children were not happy with my decision. They still are not happy as it took away their dream of having the cottage in their future with all its joy and adventures. I know their dream did not include the reality of how much work it was to maintain a beach cottage. That over-laid with the fact that they both work at very demanding jobs and have very full lives makes for a challenging reality. To my friends, the decision to sell the cottage was a disappointment and yet, every one of them understood why.

I sat with the decision and the impact of the decision – it sold in two weeks. Didn't even get beyond my putting a little sign in the yard "For Sale By Owner". Not enough time for me to get used to the idea of not having the cottage. Not enough time to let go of my relationship with Wil and the connection I have had with him in the cottage over the past 4+ years. Not enough time to let go of Berte and her fiery, strong feminism and the history she brought to the cottage.

It was a sparkly summer day in July as I sat on the cottage patio overlooking the beach in my favorite white Adirondack chair. The sky was blue, clouds were flitting by swiftly and occasionally obscuring the sun and its warmth. The tide was out, the buoys from my neighbor's crab pots were bobbing happily about a 100 feet offshore. The ferry passed by, making its regular journey bringing residents and tourists to and from the island. All was peaceful in a "norm" for the island. Except for me. As I sat there, my heart grew heavy and my breathing caught in my throat as tears clung to my eyelashes. I was grieving and I was letting go. So many thoughts raced around in my mind. I breathed deeply of the fresh sea air and continued to sit there with my thoughts and emotions.

I know that beyond this moment in time, beyond this attachment to and enjoyment of the cottage, there will be many joyful days in my new home. There will be days and events even more wonderful although different than the cottage. I need to be patient for it all to unfold. Part of my joy today is found in "paying it forward" – I am passing on the joy and sweetness of the cottage to a lovely family with three teenage girls from Redmond (same city I moved here from). They will experience many happy times there as a family, escaping the crunch and madness of life in Seattle for a quieter, peaceful place usually found only in dreams. They want to keep the cottage "as is" which warms my heart. The norm on this beach (and most beaches on Whidbey) is to tear down the small cottages and build big houses. I still treasure the simple, wonderful nature of those small beach cottages from an era long-gone.

The decision was made and two weeks after my initial grieving as I sat overlooking Columbia Beach, I handed the keys over to the new owners. As hard as that was for me, I think of Wil when he was told that his beloved cottage had been sold. He sat alone in a state-run elder care facility. His court-appointed guardian who orchestrated the sale of his permanent residence and of his cottage shared the news with him. Wil never returned to his cottage, he died less than a month after I took possession of it. It was time for him to leave this earth as there was nothing or no one he wished to remain here for. Wil was all alone.

Wil has been my Divine Mirror for the past 4 years. He has

allowed me to see in myself that which I have worked so hard not to see or acknowledge. Wil helped me understand the impact of my independence on my life. I could now see how I often seek to be alone rather than gathering with others. He helped me see that my unhappiness has nothing to do with anyone but myself. Most importantly Wil showed me that allowing life to narrow to the point where there is no joy or purpose left in it will eliminate all the possibilities. It brings you to the point of wondering if life is over and if it is time to leave this earth. I had been at that point, something I have confided to no one. I suspect more of us have those feelings than ever will admit. They are not feelings or thoughts about suicide but rather about being done and being ready to leave. I know now that I am not done and I am not ready to leave this earth.

Actively seeking to expand yourself into new learning and adventures and allowing life inside your world is what life is all about. We live in an abundant world, the possibilities for life are endless. Expanding does not come without a clear intention, hard work, much energy and complete commitment.

My journey with Wil and his cottage was difficult, time-consuming and challenging as well as costly. It was also filled with learning, laughter, people and new adventures. Very importantly, it would not have been possible if I had not asked for help and companionship. I opened the door to my life and to my heart and an abundance of life and love poured in. In its truest sense, that statement is an analogy of what I did. I opened the door of the cottage to my friends and family for nearly 4 years and they flowed in. We built bonfires, made S'mores, caught crab, capsized kayaks, built sandcastles, watched moonbeams on the water, eagles soaring high above, whales breaching, fireworks exploding and we shared wine, food, conversation - lots of conversation and an abundance of love and laughter.

Thank you Wil for being my divine mirror. What you helped me see in myself changed how I live my life. Do I see more of my family, my children and my sisters? Not really, I see them just as often as before, yet those times are happier times for me and I am at peace about it. Does it matter that I no longer have the fun beach cottage? Not really. I am as busy as I ever was, having just as much fun. As for my grandchild, I've learned that I am the magnet, she comes up to see me, not a beach or a cottage. I could live anywhere. My world of friends and connections continues to expand. My life is full and far from over. I am neither alone nor lonely.

What a wonderful thought.

Well there you go. You know I have been watching her do all that work to restore my little cottage. It was a prize when I brought it down to Columbia Beach and it had gotten into rough shape over the last decade or so. It sure shines now. She is a hard worker and not afraid of anything either - just like me. I think we are made of the same stuff.

Sure glad I didn't live in this here world today. Things are changing so fast it makes your head spin. I don't think I would have liked that much.

I was getting worried when I saw her become unhappy here. I watched Wil become so unhappy and it did not end well for him. It warms my heart to see her walk away from bad feelings and toward a place that makes her heart sing. I will always love that cottage and the beach it sits on - Columbia Beach. Now the little cottage can sit proudly in its rightful place.

As for me, I'll continue to watch folks enjoy this place. That makes me glad. I'll be sit'n as I always do - in my chair at the kitchen window - a mug of coffee in my hand and a smile upon my face, watching life happen in the world I loved most.

EPILOGUE

I have spent three years writing this book, a wonderful journey in itself. The final act of opening up my life within the cottage adventure, admitting responsibility for my life and creating space and the invitation into which life and love could flow did just that. It brought bountiful friendship, love and happiness into my life. I created room for it all and for the possibility of so much more. The joy and happiness I feel with my friends and family shines through all that I do. It is all about the journey.

I have a motto that is present in my life now, it is simply - "<u>why not</u>"?

The next time you decline an invitation, hesitate to do something, or veto an idea, stop asking yourself if it is too expensive, too time-consuming, too risky, too silly, etc. Instead, ask yourself why not? Why am I not doing this? Then seize the idea, jump in head first and do it! Carpe diem! You will be amazed at what will flow into your life when you do. I took a chance with the cottage, all the while asking myself - why not?

ABOUT THE AUTHOR

Sue Mills continues to live life on Whidbey Island. She is surrounded with new and old friends and family. She travels to "America" (the mainland) to visit her busy children and exchanges visits with her sisters. Her grandchild Aida visits often and loves time with "Momo". The new house she began after selling the cottage is now complete. Life is good . . . as it should be.

50078558R00098

Made in the USA
San Bernardino, CA
12 June 2017